We hope this book has been informative and helpful on your journey to understanding and celebrating older adults. Thank you for your interest and support!

Title: Global Politics: Exploring Diverse Systems and Ideologies
Subtitle: Understanding Political Systems, Ideologies, and Global Actors

Series: Global Perspectives: Exploring World Politics
By Jonathan A. Sinclair

Table of Contents

Introduction
The Importance of Understanding Global Politics

In an increasingly interconnected world, understanding global politics has become more important than ever. The decisions made by political leaders, the ideologies they adhere to, and the systems they govern with have far-reaching implications that impact not only nations but also individuals, communities, and the global community as a whole. This chapter aims to highlight the significance of comprehending global politics and its relevance to our lives.

1. The Interconnectedness of the World:

The first aspect that underscores the importance of understanding global politics is the interconnectedness of the world. In today's globalized era, events in one part of the world can have profound effects on distant regions. Economic crises, conflicts, pandemics, and environmental challenges all transcend borders, making it crucial for individuals to grasp the underlying political dynamics that drive these phenomena. By understanding global politics, individuals can make sense of the complex web of interactions that shape their lives and contribute to informed decision-making.

2. Shaping National Policies and International Relations:

Global politics influences national policies and international relations. Domestic policies, such as economic regulations, security measures, and social welfare systems, are shaped by both internal and external factors. Understanding the global political landscape enables citizens, policymakers, and diplomats to navigate international relations, negotiate treaties, and forge alliances effectively. Moreover, it helps governments align their policies with global goals and commitments, such as addressing climate change, promoting human rights, and combating terrorism.

3. Safeguarding Democracy and Human Rights:

Democracy and human rights are fundamental principles that many societies aspire to uphold. However, the path toward achieving and maintaining these values is not always straightforward. By studying global politics, individuals gain insights into the strengths and weaknesses of democratic systems and the challenges they face. This knowledge empowers citizens to actively participate in the democratic process, defend human rights, and hold governments accountable. It also helps identify authoritarian regimes and the tactics they employ to suppress dissent, allowing individuals to advocate for freedom and justice on a global scale.

4. Navigating Global Challenges:

Global politics plays a vital role in addressing pressing global challenges, such as climate change, poverty, terrorism, and nuclear proliferation. These complex issues require international cooperation and collective action. By understanding global politics, individuals can comprehend the various interests, ideologies, and power dynamics at play, which are crucial for finding effective solutions. It enables individuals to engage in informed discussions, contribute to policy debates, and support initiatives aimed at tackling these global challenges.

5. Cultivating Global Citizenship:

In an increasingly interconnected and diverse world, cultivating global citizenship is essential. Understanding global politics fosters a sense of shared responsibility and empathy for people from different cultures, backgrounds, and political systems. It promotes cross-cultural understanding, dialogue, and cooperation, leading to more inclusive and peaceful societies. Moreover, it helps individuals become active global citizens who are aware of their rights and responsibilities and are equipped to contribute positively to their local communities and the broader global community.

Conclusion:

Understanding global politics is crucial in today's interconnected world. It allows individuals to navigate the complexities of international relations, safeguard democracy and human rights, address global challenges, and cultivate global citizenship. By comprehending the political systems, ideologies, and actors shaping the global stage, individuals gain the knowledge and tools necessary to actively engage in shaping the future of our world. In the following chapters, we will explore major political systems, ideologies, and actors, providing a comprehensive overview of the diverse landscape of global politics.

Overview of Major Political Systems and Ideologies

To understand the complexities of global politics, it is essential to explore the major political systems and ideologies that shape the world's nations. This chapter provides an overview of these systems and ideologies, delving into their characteristics, principles, and historical contexts. By examining the diversity of political systems and ideologies, we can gain a deeper understanding of the factors influencing governance and the perspectives that drive political decision-making worldwide.

1. Democracy:

Democracy stands as one of the most prevalent political systems today, emphasizing the principles of popular sovereignty, political equality, and individual rights. This section explores the definition and core tenets of democracy, including electoral systems, democratic institutions, and the role of civil society. By examining the strengths and weaknesses of democratic governance, we can evaluate its ability to foster stable and inclusive societies while addressing the challenges and criticisms it faces.

2. Authoritarianism:

Authoritarian regimes, in contrast to democracy, concentrate political power in the hands of a single leader or a small group. This section delves into the characteristics and types of authoritarianism, exploring how these regimes consolidate power and limit civil liberties. By understanding the dynamics of authoritarian rule and the implications for human rights, we can analyze the challenges posed by these systems and their impact on domestic and international affairs.

3. Communism:

Communism has played a significant role in shaping the political landscape of the 20th century. This section provides a historical context for the emergence of communism, tracing its ideological principles and variations. By examining case studies of communist manifestations and their impact, we can analyze the historical and contemporary challenges and criticisms associated with communism. This exploration allows us to understand the legacy of communism and its influence on political systems and ideologies today.

4. Capitalism:

Capitalism, characterized by private ownership of resources and a market-driven economy, is another major political-economic system. This section delves into the principles and variations of capitalism, highlighting its focus on individual freedom, entrepreneurship, and market competition. By exploring the advantages and disadvantages of capitalism, we can evaluate its impact on economic growth, wealth distribution, and social welfare, and examine the interplay between capitalism and democracy.

5. Socialism:

Socialism, rooted in the principles of equality, collective ownership, and redistribution of wealth, offers an alternative perspective to capitalism. This section explores the origins, principles, and variations of socialism, highlighting its emphasis on social justice and public ownership. By analyzing the impact of socialism on economic systems, social welfare, and political governance, we can assess its strengths, challenges, and influence on contemporary political ideologies.

6. Other Political Ideologies:

Beyond the major systems discussed above, this section explores other significant political ideologies and movements that shape global politics. Liberalism, conservatism, environmentalism, and religious fundamentalism are among the ideologies considered. By examining the origins, principles, and influence of these ideologies, we gain insight into the diverse perspectives and competing visions that impact political decision-making and societal development.

Conclusion:

Understanding the major political systems and ideologies is crucial for comprehending the dynamics of global politics. By exploring democracy, authoritarianism, communism, capitalism, socialism, and other political ideologies, we gain a comprehensive overview of the diverse landscape that shapes governance and policy-making worldwide. This knowledge equips us with the tools to critically analyze the strengths, weaknesses, and impacts of these systems and ideologies, enabling us to navigate the complex world of global politics with greater insight and understanding. In the following chapters, we will delve deeper into specific aspects and manifestations of these systems and ideologies, allowing for a more comprehensive exploration of their histories, contemporary manifestations, and implications for global affairs.

Actors on the Global Stage

Global politics is a complex arena where numerous actors exert influence and shape the course of international affairs. Understanding the various actors involved is crucial for comprehending the dynamics of global governance, decision-making processes, and the pursuit of national and global interests. This chapter provides an exploration of the key actors on the global stage, including states, international organizations, non-state actors, and transnational corporations. By examining their roles, motivations, and interactions, we can gain insights into the multifaceted nature of global politics.

1. States:

States are central actors in global politics, representing the interests and aspirations of their populations. This section explores the role of states in the international system, examining their sovereignty, power dynamics, and foreign policies. By analyzing the motivations and strategies of states, we can better understand their interactions, including alliances, rivalries, and conflicts. Additionally, we explore the role of diplomacy and statecraft in shaping global relations.

2. International Organizations:

International organizations play a significant role in facilitating cooperation and addressing global challenges. This section examines the role and significance of international organizations, such as the United Nations, World Trade Organization, and regional bodies. We explore their functions, decision-making processes, and contributions to global governance. Additionally, we consider the challenges and opportunities faced by international organizations in addressing complex issues such as climate change, peacekeeping, and humanitarian crises.

3. Non-State Actors:

Beyond states and international organizations, non-state actors have gained prominence in global politics. This section explores the role of non-state actors, including non-governmental organizations (NGOs), advocacy groups, and grassroots movements. We examine how these actors shape global agendas, mobilize public opinion, and advocate for specific causes, such as human rights, environmental protection, and social justice. Additionally, we discuss the impact of social media and technology in empowering non-state actors and facilitating global activism.

4. Transnational Corporations:

Transnational corporations (TNCs) exert significant economic influence and shape global politics through their operations, investments, and interactions with states and international organizations. This section examines the role of TNCs in the global economy, exploring their motivations, impact on labor and the environment, and their relationship with host states. We also consider the growing calls for corporate social responsibility and the challenges of regulating TNCs in a globalized world.

5. Supranational Entities:

Supranational entities, such as the European Union, are unique actors on the global stage. This section explores the evolution, functions, and challenges faced by supranational entities. We examine how supranational governance structures impact the sovereignty of member states, promote economic integration, and facilitate decision-making in areas such as trade, security, and migration. Additionally, we discuss the implications of regionalism and the rise of regional organizations in global politics.

6. Civil Society and Global Citizenship:

Civil society and global citizenship have gained increasing relevance in global politics. This section examines the role of civil society actors, including academics, journalists, and social movements, in shaping global agendas and holding governments and international organizations accountable. We explore the concept of global citizenship and its potential to foster cross-border solidarity, activism, and collaboration in addressing global challenges.

Conclusion:

Understanding the actors on the global stage is essential for comprehending the dynamics of global politics. States, international organizations, non-state actors, and transnational corporations each play distinct roles and have unique motivations and interactions. By examining their roles and relationships, we gain insights into the complex web of actors that shape global governance, policy-making, and the pursuit of national and global interests. In the following chapters, we will delve deeper into specific case studies and examine how these actors influence and shape global politics in different contexts.

Chapter 1: Democratic Governance
Definition and Principles of Democracy

Democratic governance is a cornerstone of many contemporary societies, emphasizing principles of popular participation, political equality, and respect for individual rights. This chapter explores the definition and key principles of democracy, providing a comprehensive understanding of its foundations. By delving into the principles that underpin democratic governance, we can better grasp its significance, strengths, and challenges in modern political systems.

1. Understanding Democracy:

Democracy, derived from the Greek words "demos" (people) and "kratos" (rule), can be broadly defined as a system of government where power resides with the people, who exercise their authority through fair and free elections. This section explores the different elements that characterize democratic governance, including political participation, electoral processes, and the rule of law. By understanding the core components of democracy, we can establish a solid foundation for further analysis.

2. Principles of Democracy:

2.1. Popular Sovereignty:

One of the fundamental principles of democracy is popular sovereignty, which emphasizes that political power ultimately resides with the people. This section explores the concept of popular sovereignty, highlighting how it ensures that the government's legitimacy derives from the consent of the governed. We discuss the importance of citizen participation, public deliberation, and inclusive decision-making processes in upholding popular sovereignty.

2.2. Political Equality:

Political equality is another central principle of democracy, advocating for equal rights and opportunities for all individuals to participate in the political process. This section examines the concept of political equality, exploring the importance of universal suffrage, equal representation, and non-discrimination in democratic societies. We also address challenges related to marginalized groups, voter suppression, and ensuring equitable political participation.

2.3. Rule of Law and Human Rights:

Democracy is closely tied to the rule of law and the protection of human rights. This section explores the relationship between democracy, the rule of law, and human rights, emphasizing the importance of legal frameworks, independent judiciary, and respect for civil liberties. We discuss the role of constitutionalism, checks and balances, and the promotion and protection of human rights in democratic governance.

2.4. Pluralism and Tolerance:

Pluralism and tolerance are essential principles that promote diversity, inclusivity, and the accommodation of different viewpoints in democratic societies. This section explores the concept of pluralism, highlighting its significance in fostering open dialogue, peaceful coexistence, and robust civil society. We address the challenges of balancing competing interests, managing conflicts, and upholding tolerance in diverse democratic societies.

2.5. Accountability and Transparency:

Accountability and transparency are vital pillars of democratic governance, ensuring that those in power are answerable to the people. This section examines mechanisms of accountability, including free media, independent oversight institutions, and the role of civil society. We also discuss the importance of transparency in promoting trust, combating corruption, and enhancing public participation in decision-making processes.

Conclusion:

Understanding the definition and principles of democracy provides a solid framework for analyzing democratic governance. The principles of popular sovereignty, political equality, rule of law, human rights, pluralism, tolerance, and accountability lay the foundation for democratic systems. By exploring these principles, we gain insight into the strengths and values that democratic governance upholds. However, challenges such as voter apathy, polarization, and the erosion of democratic norms remind us of the ongoing efforts needed to protect and strengthen democratic institutions. In the following sections, we will delve deeper into the electoral systems, democratic institutions, strengths, challenges, and criticisms associated with democratic governance.

Central to democratic governance are electoral systems and democratic institutions that ensure fair and representative processes for decision-making. This chapter examines the different types of electoral systems and the role of democratic institutions in upholding the principles of democracy. By exploring the intricacies of electoral systems and democratic institutions, we can gain a comprehensive understanding of their impact on democratic governance.

1. Electoral Systems:

1.1. Plurality/Majority Systems:

Plurality/majority systems, such as First-Past-The-Post and two-round systems, are commonly used electoral systems worldwide. This section explores the characteristics of plurality/majority systems, including single-member districts, winner-takes-all outcomes, and the impact on political parties. We discuss the strengths and weaknesses of these systems, such as their simplicity, representation of geographic constituencies, and potential for excluding minority voices.

1.2. Proportional Representation Systems:

Proportional representation systems, such as List Proportional Representation and Single Transferable Vote, aim to ensure a fairer distribution of seats based on the proportion of votes received by each political party. This section delves into the principles and variations of proportional representation systems, examining their impact on political party representation, voter choice, and inclusivity. We discuss the strengths and weaknesses of proportional representation systems, including their potential to foster multi-party systems and accommodate diverse political preferences.

1.3. Mixed Electoral Systems:

Mixed electoral systems combine elements of both plurality/majority and proportional representation systems. This section explores the features and variations of mixed electoral systems, including parallel systems and compensatory mechanisms. We discuss the strengths and weaknesses of mixed systems, considering their ability to balance constituency representation and proportional outcomes.

2. Democratic Institutions:

2.1. Executive Branch:

The executive branch of government, headed by the president or prime minister, plays a crucial role in democratic governance. This section examines the functions and responsibilities of the executive branch, including the separation of powers, checks and balances, and the role of executive leadership in policy-making and implementation. We discuss the importance of executive accountability, transparency, and the impact of presidential versus parliamentary systems.

2.2. Legislative Branch:

The legislative branch, comprising national and subnational parliaments, is a key democratic institution responsible for lawmaking, representation, and oversight. This section explores the structure and functions of the legislative branch, including the role of political parties, committee systems, and the legislative process. We discuss the challenges of legislative effectiveness, inclusivity, and the representation of diverse interests.

2.3. Judicial Branch:

An independent judiciary is essential for upholding the rule of law and protecting individual rights in a democratic society. This section examines the role of the judicial branch in democratic governance, exploring judicial independence, the interpretation of laws, and the protection of civil liberties. We discuss the challenges of judicial activism, judicial accountability, and the relationship between the judiciary and other branches of government.

2.4. Civil Society and Media:

Democratic institutions are reinforced by the active participation of civil society organizations and a free and independent media. This section explores the role of civil society organizations, including advocacy groups, non-governmental organizations, and social movements, in promoting accountability, transparency, and citizen engagement. We also discuss the importance of a free and independent media in facilitating informed public discourse and holding power-holders accountable.

Conclusion:

Electoral systems and democratic institutions are crucial components of democratic governance, ensuring fair and representative decision-making processes. By examining different electoral systems, such as plurality/majority, proportional representation, and mixed systems, we gain insight into their strengths and weaknesses in fostering political representation and inclusivity. Additionally, understanding the role of democratic institutions, including the executive, legislative, judicial branches, civil society, and media, provides a comprehensive view of the checks and balances necessary for upholding democratic principles. In the following sections, we will explore the strengths, challenges, and criticisms associated with democratic governance, further examining its impact on societies worldwide.

Strengths of Democratic Governance

Democratic governance offers numerous strengths that make it an appealing system for societies around the world. This chapter explores the strengths of democratic governance, highlighting its ability to promote political participation, protect individual rights, foster stability, and enhance societal development. By understanding and analyzing these strengths, we can gain a deeper appreciation for the merits of democratic governance.

1. Political Participation:

One of the key strengths of democratic governance is its emphasis on political participation. Democratic systems provide opportunities for citizens to engage in political processes, express their preferences, and contribute to decision-making. This section examines the importance of citizen participation in democratic governance, exploring mechanisms such as elections, referendums, and public consultations. We discuss how political participation enhances legitimacy, accountability, and representation in democratic systems.

2. Protection of Individual Rights:

Democratic governance prioritizes the protection of individual rights and liberties. This section explores how democratic systems safeguard civil, political, and social rights, including freedom of speech, assembly, and association. We discuss the role of independent judiciaries, constitutional frameworks, and human rights institutions in upholding individual rights within democratic societies. Additionally, we address the significance of inclusive and non-discriminatory policies in ensuring equal protection for all citizens.

3. Peaceful Transition of Power:

One of the notable strengths of democratic governance is its ability to facilitate the peaceful transition of power. Through regular elections and the acceptance of election outcomes, democratic systems provide a peaceful mechanism for transferring authority from one government to another. This section examines the significance of peaceful transitions of power in maintaining political stability and avoiding authoritarian rule or violent conflicts. We discuss case studies of successful transitions and the role of democratic institutions in ensuring stability during political transitions.

4. Checks and Balances:

Democratic governance incorporates a system of checks and balances to prevent the concentration of power. This section explores the strengths of checks and balances mechanisms, including the separation of powers, independent judiciary, and legislative oversight. We discuss how these mechanisms help prevent abuse of power, corruption, and ensure accountability among different branches of government. Additionally, we address the role of civil society organizations, media, and public scrutiny in holding power-holders accountable.

5. Responsive and Accountable Governance:

Democratic systems prioritize responsive and accountable governance, ensuring that leaders are accountable to their constituents. This section examines the strengths of responsive governance, including policy responsiveness, transparency, and public engagement. We discuss how democratic institutions foster open dialogue, encourage policy responsiveness, and enable citizens to voice their concerns and preferences. Additionally, we address the role of political parties and electoral competition in promoting accountability.

6. Socioeconomic Development:

Democratic governance has shown a correlation with socioeconomic development. This section explores the strengths of democratic systems in fostering economic growth, social welfare, and human development. We examine the role of democratic institutions in promoting economic policies that prioritize inclusive growth, investment in education and healthcare, and poverty reduction. We discuss case studies of countries that have achieved significant socioeconomic progress through democratic governance.

Conclusion:

Democratic governance possesses numerous strengths that make it an appealing system for societies worldwide. Through political participation, the protection of individual rights, peaceful transitions of power, checks and balances, responsive governance, and socioeconomic development, democratic systems offer a framework for inclusive and accountable governance. However, it is important to acknowledge the challenges and limitations that democracies face. In the following sections, we will delve into the criticisms and challenges of democratic governance to provide a comprehensive understanding of its complexities.

While democratic governance offers numerous strengths, it is not without its challenges and criticisms. This chapter delves into the complex landscape of challenges and criticisms faced by democratic systems. By examining these issues, we can gain a deeper understanding of the limitations and areas where democratic governance may fall short. It is through recognizing and addressing these challenges that democracies can evolve and strengthen over time.

1. Political Polarization:

One of the major challenges facing democratic systems is political polarization. This section explores the causes and consequences of political polarization, including the rise of extremist ideologies, erosion of trust in institutions, and the inability to find common ground. We discuss the impact of polarization on political discourse, decision-making, and the potential for social divisions. Additionally, we explore strategies for mitigating polarization and fostering constructive dialogue.

2. Voter Apathy and Disengagement:

Voter apathy and disengagement pose significant challenges to democratic governance. This section examines the causes and implications of voter apathy, including disillusionment with the political process, lack of trust in politicians, and barriers to participation. We discuss the impact of low voter turnout on representation, legitimacy, and the potential for populist movements to exploit disengaged populations. We also explore strategies for increasing voter engagement and revitalizing democratic participation.

3. Corruption and Money in Politics:

Corruption and the influence of money in politics undermine the integrity and fairness of democratic systems. This section explores the challenges posed by corruption, including the distortion of public policy, unequal access to political power, and erosion of public trust. We discuss the role of campaign finance regulations, transparency measures, and anti-corruption initiatives in combating these challenges. Additionally, we address the importance of strong institutions and independent oversight in ensuring accountability.

4. Minority Rights and Inclusivity:

Democratic governance must address the challenge of protecting and promoting the rights of minority groups. This section examines the importance of inclusivity and the challenges faced by marginalized communities, including ethnic, religious, and gender minorities. We discuss the potential for majority rule to neglect minority rights and the need for affirmative measures, representation, and inclusive policies to address these challenges. Additionally, we explore the tension between majority rule and minority rights in democratic decision-making.

5. Democratic Backsliding and Authoritarianism:

Democracies are not immune to the threat of democratic backsliding and the rise of authoritarianism. This section examines the challenges posed by the erosion of democratic norms, attacks on independent institutions, and the concentration of power. We discuss case studies of democratic backsliding, the role of populist movements, and the potential for democratic erosion. We also explore strategies for safeguarding democratic institutions and addressing the challenges of authoritarian tendencies.

6. Globalization and Complexity:

The complexities of globalization pose challenges to democratic governance. This section explores how global interconnectedness, economic interdependence, and technological advancements impact democratic decision-making and policy implementation. We discuss the challenges of balancing national interests with global cooperation, addressing transnational issues, and managing the impact of globalization on domestic economies and societies.

Conclusion:

Challenges and criticisms are inherent in democratic governance, and addressing them is essential for the long-term vitality and effectiveness of democratic systems. By acknowledging the challenges of political polarization, voter apathy, corruption, minority rights, democratic backsliding, and globalization, societies can work towards strengthening democratic institutions and practices. It is through constructive dialogue, inclusive policies, and continuous efforts to address these challenges that democracies can evolve and adapt to the changing needs of their societies. In the following sections, we will explore the history and contemporary manifestations of authoritarian regimes and their comparison with democratic governance.

Characteristics and Types of Authoritarianism

Authoritarian regimes represent an alternative form of governance that stands in contrast to democratic systems. This chapter explores the characteristics and types of authoritarianism, providing an understanding of the key features that define such regimes. By examining different manifestations of authoritarianism, we can gain insights into the mechanisms through which power is consolidated and controlled, and the implications for governance, human rights, and civil liberties.

1. Definition and Key Characteristics of Authoritarianism:

This section provides an overview of authoritarianism, defining it as a system of government where power is concentrated in the hands of a single leader, ruling elite, or political party. We discuss the key characteristics that distinguish authoritarian regimes, including limited political freedoms, restricted civil liberties, centralized decision-making, and a lack of checks and balances. Additionally, we explore the role of ideology, propaganda, and repression in maintaining authoritarian control.

2. Types of Authoritarian Regimes:

2.1. Totalitarianism:

Totalitarian regimes represent the most extreme form of authoritarianism, characterized by absolute control over all aspects of society. This section delves into the features of totalitarian regimes, including an all-encompassing ideology, pervasive state surveillance, suppression of dissent, and the manipulation of information and propaganda. We discuss case studies of historical totalitarian regimes and their impact on governance, society, and human rights.

2.2. Military Juntas and Dictatorships:

Military juntas and dictatorships are authoritarian regimes where power is held by the military or a single ruler. This section examines the characteristics of military juntas and dictatorships, including the concentration of power, the role of the military in politics, and the absence of democratic institutions. We discuss case studies of military juntas and dictatorships, exploring their impact on governance, stability, and human rights.

2.3. Single-Party States:

Single-party states are characterized by the dominance of a single political party that maintains a monopoly on power. This section explores the features of single-party states, including the suppression of political opposition, limited political pluralism, and the control of state institutions by the ruling party. We discuss case studies of single-party states, examining their governance models, ideological foundations, and the challenges they pose to democratic values.

2.4. Personalistic Authoritarianism:

Personalistic authoritarianism revolves around a single charismatic leader who holds significant power and influence. This section delves into the characteristics of personalistic authoritarian regimes, including the cult of personality, the centralization of power around the leader, and the absence of institutional checks. We discuss case studies of personalistic authoritarian regimes, exploring their impact on governance, patronage systems, and political succession.

3. Hybrid Regimes:

Hybrid regimes represent a combination of authoritarian and democratic elements, blurring the lines between the two systems. This section examines the characteristics of hybrid regimes, including limited political competition, controlled media, and the manipulation of elections. We discuss the challenges posed by hybrid regimes, their impact on governance and civil society, and the complexities of transitioning to democracy.

4. Comparative Analysis of Authoritarian Regimes:

In this section, we conduct a comparative analysis of different types of authoritarian regimes, highlighting their similarities and differences. We explore factors such as the degree of repression, ideological foundations, economic policies, and international relations. Additionally, we discuss the challenges faced by authoritarian regimes, including internal dissent, legitimacy concerns, and the potential for political instability.

Conclusion:

Authoritarian regimes exhibit various characteristics and types, each with its distinct features and implications for governance and society. By understanding the defining characteristics of authoritarianism and analyzing the different types of regimes, we can gain insights into the mechanisms through which power is consolidated and controlled. However, it is important to recognize the limitations and challenges posed by authoritarian systems, including restrictions on political freedoms, human rights abuses, and the lack of accountability and transparency. In the following sections, we will delve deeper into the suppression of dissent and limitations on civil liberties within authoritarian regimes, as well as their implications for human rights.

Authoritarian regimes are characterized by the concentration and consolidation of power in the hands of a single leader, ruling elite, or political party. This chapter explores the mechanisms through which power is consolidated within authoritarian regimes, shedding light on the strategies, institutions, and tactics employed to maintain control. By understanding the consolidation of power in authoritarian regimes, we can gain insights into their governance structures, challenges to political plurality, and the implications for society and human rights.

1. Centralization of Political Power:

Centralization of political power is a fundamental characteristic of authoritarian regimes. This section explores the mechanisms through which power is concentrated, including the establishment of strong executive authority, the weakening of checks and balances, and the manipulation of legal and institutional frameworks. We discuss case studies of authoritarian regimes, examining their methods of centralizing power and the consequences for governance.

2. Suppression of Political Opposition:

Authoritarian regimes employ various tactics to suppress political opposition and maintain control. This section delves into the strategies used to silence dissent, including censorship, repression, and the use of security forces to stifle opposition movements. We explore the role of surveillance, propaganda, and control of the media in suppressing dissent. Additionally, we discuss the impact of these tactics on civil liberties, political pluralism, and democratic values.

3. Cult of Personality and Ideological Control:

Many authoritarian regimes cultivate a cult of personality around the leader or ruling elite to legitimize their authority. This section examines the role of personality cults and ideological control in consolidating power. We discuss how leaders use propaganda, symbolism, and mass mobilization to foster loyalty and maintain control. Additionally, we explore the manipulation of ideology to justify repressive measures and reinforce the regime's narrative.

4. Patronage Networks and Co-optation:

Authoritarian regimes often rely on patronage networks and co-optation strategies to maintain loyalty and control. This section explores how leaders build networks of patronage, rewarding supporters with political positions, economic benefits, and other privileges. We discuss the impact of these networks on governance, corruption, and the erosion of institutional integrity. Additionally, we examine the co-optation of key societal groups, such as the military, business elites, and religious institutions.

5. State Surveillance and Control:

State surveillance and control are key mechanisms used by authoritarian regimes to monitor and suppress dissent. This section examines the role of surveillance technologies, intelligence agencies, and informants in maintaining control. We discuss the implications of mass surveillance on privacy, freedom of expression, and the potential chilling effect on political activism. Additionally, we explore the use of modern technologies and digital censorship to control information flow and restrict access to dissenting voices.

6. Economic Control and Rent-Seeking:

Authoritarian regimes often exercise significant control over the economy as a means to consolidate power. This section explores how economic control and rent-seeking practices are employed to maintain loyalty, reward supporters, and control resources. We discuss the impact of economic control on wealth distribution, corruption, and the suppression of economic competition. Additionally, we address the challenges of sustainable economic development within authoritarian regimes.

Conclusion:

The consolidation of power in authoritarian regimes involves various strategies and tactics aimed at maintaining control, suppressing dissent, and perpetuating the ruling elite's authority. Through centralization of political power, suppression of political opposition, cults of personality, patronage networks, state surveillance, and economic control, authoritarian regimes seek to solidify their grip on power. However, these consolidation efforts come at the expense of civil liberties, political pluralism, and democratic values. In the following sections, we will examine the implications of authoritarianism on human rights and the limitations it poses for societal development.

Suppression of Dissent and Limitations on Civil Liberties

Authoritarian regimes are known for their suppression of dissent and restrictions on civil liberties. This chapter examines the methods and mechanisms through which authoritarian regimes curtail political freedoms, stifle opposition, and control society. By understanding the tactics used to suppress dissent and limit civil liberties, we can shed light on the challenges faced by individuals and societies living under such regimes, as well as the broader implications for human rights and democratic values.

1. Censorship and Media Control:

Censorship is a prevalent tool used by authoritarian regimes to control information flow and manipulate public opinion. This section explores the various forms of censorship employed, including state control of media outlets, internet restrictions, and the suppression of independent journalism. We examine the impact of media control on freedom of expression, access to information, and the ability of citizens to hold the regime accountable.

2. Repression and Political Persecution:

Authoritarian regimes often resort to repression and political persecution to quash dissent and silence opposition. This section delves into the methods of repression employed, such as arbitrary arrests, torture, extrajudicial killings, and enforced disappearances. We discuss the impact of repression on individual freedoms, the fear it instills in society, and the long-lasting psychological effects on victims and their families.

3. Surveillance and Monitoring:

State surveillance is a key tool used by authoritarian regimes to monitor the activities of their citizens, suppress dissent, and maintain control. This section explores the extent of surveillance practices, including mass surveillance programs, monitoring of communication channels, and the use of technology for citizen tracking. We discuss the implications of pervasive surveillance on privacy, freedom of association, and the chilling effect it has on political activism.

4. Restrictions on Freedom of Assembly and Association:

Authoritarian regimes often impose severe restrictions on freedom of assembly and association to prevent the formation of organized opposition. This section examines the limitations placed on public gatherings, demonstrations, and the functioning of civil society organizations. We discuss the consequences of these restrictions on collective action, the stifling of grassroots movements, and the erosion of spaces for civic engagement.

5. Constraints on Political Participation and Elections:

Authoritarian regimes employ various tactics to control political participation and manipulate electoral processes. This section explores the ways in which regimes restrict political competition, manipulate electoral laws, and engage in voter intimidation. We discuss the impact of these constraints on the legitimacy of elections, the representation of diverse voices, and the erosion of democratic principles.

6. Suppression of Academic Freedom and Intellectual Dissent:

Authoritarian regimes often target intellectuals, academics, and educational institutions as a means to control narratives and restrict intellectual dissent. This section examines the suppression of academic freedom, including censorship of research, control over educational curricula, and limitations on freedom of thought and expression within educational institutions. We discuss the consequences of stifling intellectual dissent and the implications for societal progress and innovation.

Conclusion:

The suppression of dissent and limitations on civil liberties are defining features of authoritarian regimes. Through censorship, repression, surveillance, restrictions on freedom of assembly and association, constraints on political participation, and suppression of academic freedom, these regimes aim to maintain control, silence opposition, and restrict the rights of individuals and society as a whole. However, these tactics come at the expense of human rights, democratic values, and societal progress. In the following sections, we will analyze the implications of these suppressive measures for human rights abuses, the rule of law, and the prospects for democratic change.

Authoritarian regimes are notorious for their disregard of human rights, as they prioritize maintaining power and control over the well-being and freedoms of their citizens. This chapter explores the profound implications of authoritarianism on human rights, examining the ways in which these regimes violate and suppress fundamental rights and freedoms. By understanding the impact of authoritarian rule on human rights, we can shed light on the urgent need for international advocacy and support for those affected by such regimes.

1. Violations of Freedom of Expression and Press Freedom:

Authoritarian regimes often impose severe restrictions on freedom of expression and press freedom. This section examines how these regimes silence dissenting voices, censor the media, and control the dissemination of information. We discuss the impact of these violations on individuals' ability to express themselves freely, the stifling of public debate and discourse, and the erosion of democratic values.

2. Repression of Political Activism and Civil Society:

Authoritarian regimes employ various tactics to suppress political activism and undermine civil society organizations. This section explores how these regimes target human rights defenders, activists, and non-governmental organizations. We discuss the consequences of such repression on the ability of individuals and groups to advocate for human rights, the impact on social movements, and the shrinking space for civil society.

3. Restrictions on Freedom of Assembly and Association:

Authoritarian regimes often impose stringent restrictions on freedom of assembly and association to prevent the formation of organized opposition. This section examines how these regimes curtail the rights of individuals and groups to gather, demonstrate, and form associations. We discuss the implications of these restrictions on collective action, the stifling of grassroots movements, and the erosion of spaces for civic engagement.

4. Abuse of State Power and Rule of Law:

Authoritarian regimes frequently abuse state power and manipulate the rule of law to suppress dissent and maintain control. This section explores the ways in which these regimes undermine judicial independence, engage in arbitrary arrests and detentions, and subject individuals to unfair trials. We discuss the erosion of the rule of law, the lack of accountability for human rights violations, and the devastating impact on individuals' lives.

5. Torture, Ill-Treatment, and Extra-Judicial Killings:

Authoritarian regimes have a notorious track record of resorting to torture, ill-treatment, and extra-judicial killings to maintain control and instill fear. This section examines the widespread use of torture and ill-treatment within these regimes' detention centers, as well as the targeted killings of political opponents and dissidents. We discuss the physical and psychological consequences of these human rights abuses and the urgent need for accountability.

6. Implications for Marginalized Groups:

Authoritarian regimes often exacerbate human rights abuses against marginalized groups, including ethnic and religious minorities, women, LGBTQ+ individuals, and indigenous communities. This section examines the specific challenges faced by these groups under authoritarian rule, such as discrimination, persecution, and violence. We discuss the importance of intersectionality in addressing human rights violations and the need for inclusive advocacy.

Conclusion:

Authoritarian regimes pose a severe threat to human rights, with their violations and suppression of fundamental freedoms impacting individuals, communities, and society as a whole. Through restrictions on freedom of expression and press freedom, repression of political activism, limitations on freedom of assembly and association, abuse of state power and the rule of law, and the widespread use of torture and ill-treatment, these regimes trample on the principles of human rights and dignity. It is crucial to advocate for the protection and promotion of human rights in the face of authoritarianism, standing in solidarity with those affected and striving for a more just and inclusive world.

Communism is a political ideology that has had a significant impact on global politics. This chapter explores the historical context and origins of communism, tracing its development from early theoretical foundations to its real-world manifestations. By understanding the historical roots of communism, we can gain insights into its ideological principles, its goals, and the various challenges and criticisms it has faced throughout history.

1. Predecessors and Early Influences:

To comprehend the historical context of communism, it is essential to explore the intellectual and social currents that shaped its emergence. This section examines the influences of early thinkers, such as Karl Marx and Friedrich Engels, and their engagement with the social, economic, and political issues of their time. We discuss the impact of the Industrial Revolution, the rise of capitalism, and the Enlightenment era on the development of communist thought.

2. The Communist Manifesto:

The publication of "The Communist Manifesto" in 1848 by Marx and Engels marked a significant milestone in the history of communism. This section analyzes the manifesto's content, its core principles, and its critique of capitalism and class struggle. We delve into the historical circumstances that influenced its creation, the reception of the manifesto, and its lasting impact on subsequent communist movements.

3. Early Experiments: Paris Commune and Russian Revolution:

Communism found its earliest practical expressions in events such as the Paris Commune of 1871 and the Russian Revolution of 1917. This section explores these historical episodes and their role in shaping the evolution of communism. We examine the motivations, successes, and failures of these early experiments in establishing communist governance, the challenges they faced, and the lessons learned for future communist movements.

4. Marxist-Leninism and the Soviet Model:

The rise of the Soviet Union under the leadership of Vladimir Lenin and the subsequent development of Marxist-Leninism significantly impacted the trajectory of communism. This section examines the principles of Marxist-Leninist ideology, the consolidation of power under Lenin and later Joseph Stalin, and the establishment of the Soviet model of communism. We discuss the economic, social, and political aspects of the Soviet system and its influence on global communism.

5. Variations and Divergence: Maoism and Other Communist Movements:

Communism has taken on various forms and interpretations in different parts of the world. This section explores Maoism as an important variation of communism, focusing on its development in China under Mao Zedong. Additionally, we examine other significant communist movements and their unique characteristics, including those in Cuba, Vietnam, and North Korea. We discuss the factors that led to these variations and the challenges they faced in implementing communist ideals.

6. Decline of Communism in the 20th Century:

The 20th century witnessed the rise and decline of communism in many countries. This section examines the factors that contributed to the decline of communism, including internal challenges, external pressures, and the changing global political landscape. We analyze the collapse of the Soviet Union, the transition of former communist countries to other political systems, and the legacy of communism in the modern world.

Conclusion:

Understanding the historical context and origins of communism provides valuable insights into its development as a political ideology. From the early influences on Marx and Engels to the practical implementations of communism in various countries, tracing its evolution allows us to grasp the complexities, achievements, and shortcomings of this ideology. By critically examining its historical foundations, we can gain a deeper understanding of communism's principles, its relevance in contemporary global politics, and the ongoing debates surrounding its viability and efficacy.

The ideology of communism has evolved over time, giving rise to various interpretations and adaptations. This chapter explores the ideological principles of communism and the different variations that have emerged in different contexts. By examining these principles and variations, we can gain a comprehensive understanding of the diverse manifestations of communism and the factors that have shaped its evolution.

1. Core Principles of Communism:

To understand the ideological foundations of communism, it is essential to explore its core principles. This section delves into the key tenets of communism, including the abolition of private property, collective ownership of means of production, and the goal of establishing a classless society. We discuss the concept of class struggle, the critique of capitalism, and the vision of a socialist society based on equality and cooperation.

2. Marxism and Scientific Socialism:

Marxism, developed by Karl Marx and Friedrich Engels, forms the basis for many communist ideologies. This section explores the key principles of Marxism, including historical materialism, the dialectical understanding of social change, and the role of the working class in revolutionary transformation. We discuss the concept of surplus value, the critique of bourgeois society, and the ultimate aim of establishing a communist society.

3. Leninism and Vanguard Party:

Leninism, as developed by Vladimir Lenin, introduced several adaptations to Marxist theory. This section examines the concept of the vanguard party, which is seen as the leading force in the revolutionary struggle. We discuss Lenin's theories on imperialism, the role of the proletariat and peasantry, and the concept of democratic centralism. We also explore the impact of Leninism on the practice of communism in the Soviet Union and beyond.

4. Maoism and Mass Line:

Mao Zedong's contributions to communist theory, known as Maoism, introduced additional variations to the ideology. This section explores Mao's emphasis on the importance of the masses and the concept of the mass line, which advocates for a close connection between the party and the people. We discuss Mao's theories on protracted people's war, rural revolution, and the role of peasants in the revolutionary process.

5. National Communism and Cultural Contexts:

Communism has taken on different forms and adaptations in various cultural and national contexts. This section examines national communism, exploring examples such as Titoism in Yugoslavia, Ho Chi Minh's version of communism in Vietnam, and Castroism in Cuba. We discuss how these variations incorporated unique cultural, historical, and geopolitical factors into their communist ideologies.

6. Contemporary Variations and Debates:

In the contemporary era, communism continues to evolve and adapt to changing political landscapes. This section explores modern variations of communism, such as Eurocommunism, democratic socialism, and neo-Maoism. We discuss the debates and tensions surrounding these variations, including the balance between revolutionary transformation and democratic governance, the role of markets and private property, and the relationship between communism and other ideological frameworks.

Conclusion:

The ideological principles of communism form the foundation for various interpretations and adaptations that have emerged throughout history. From the core principles of Marxism to the variations introduced by Leninism, Maoism, and national communism, communism has evolved in response to different contexts and challenges. By examining these ideological principles and variations, we gain a deeper understanding of the complexities, debates, and transformations within the communist ideology. This understanding is crucial for comprehending the diverse manifestations of communism in different countries and its continued relevance in contemporary global politics.

Case Studies: Communist Manifestations and Their Impact

The evolution of communism has resulted in various real-world manifestations with distinct impacts on societies and global politics. This chapter examines key case studies that exemplify the implementation of communist ideologies in different contexts. By analyzing these case studies, we can gain insights into the practical challenges, achievements, and consequences of communist governance and its impact on social, economic, and political systems.

1. Soviet Union: The Birth of a Communist State:

The Soviet Union, established after the Russian Revolution, represents one of the most significant case studies in communist history. This section explores the early years of the Soviet Union under Lenin and the subsequent leadership of Joseph Stalin. We examine the establishment of a planned economy, collectivization of agriculture, the Great Purge, and the impact of the Soviet Union on global geopolitics. We also discuss the social and cultural transformations that occurred under communist rule.

2. China: Mao's Communist Revolution:

China's communist revolution led by Mao Zedong provides another crucial case study. This section explores the rise of the Chinese Communist Party, the Long March, and the establishment of the People's Republic of China. We analyze Mao's policies, including the Great Leap Forward, the Cultural Revolution, and the implementation of socialist ideals. We examine the social, economic, and political consequences of Mao's rule and the long-term impact on China's trajectory.

3. Cuba: Fidel Castro's Revolution:

Cuba's communist revolution, led by Fidel Castro, presents a case study of communism in a Latin American context. This section examines the factors that led to the Cuban Revolution, Castro's rise to power, and the establishment of a socialist state. We discuss the nationalization of industries, the relationship with the Soviet Union, the Cuban Missile Crisis, and the enduring legacy of Castro's regime. We analyze the socio-economic developments and challenges faced by Cuba under communist governance.

4. Eastern Bloc: Communism in Eastern Europe:

The communist regimes in Eastern Europe, often referred to as the Eastern Bloc, offer an important case study in understanding the diverse manifestations of communism. This section explores countries such as East Germany, Poland, Hungary, and Czechoslovakia, analyzing the establishment of communist governments, the Soviet influence, and the challenges faced by these regimes. We discuss the social control mechanisms, economic structures, and eventual transitions away from communism in the region.

5. North Korea: Juche Ideology and Totalitarian Rule:

North Korea presents a unique case study of communism under the leadership of the Kim dynasty. This section examines the implementation of Juche ideology, characterized by self-reliance and a cult of personality. We analyze the totalitarian control exerted by the regime, the state-controlled economy, and the impact on North Korean society. We also discuss the geopolitical challenges and the consequences of North Korea's isolation from the international community.

6. Comparative Analysis and Lessons Learned:

In this section, we provide a comparative analysis of the case studies presented and draw insights from the various communist manifestations. We discuss commonalities and differences in policies, strategies, and outcomes across different contexts. We analyze the social, economic, and political implications of communist governance, including its successes, failures, and long-term legacies. We also consider the international ramifications and ideological debates surrounding communism.

Conclusion:

The case studies of communist manifestations explored in this chapter offer valuable insights into the practical challenges, achievements, and consequences of implementing communist ideologies. From the Soviet Union to China, Cuba, Eastern Europe, and North Korea, these case studies demonstrate the diverse ways in which communism has been practiced and its impact on societies and global politics. By examining these case studies, we can gain a deeper understanding of the complexities, achievements, and shortcomings of communist governance, informing our analysis of its historical and contemporary significance.

Contemporary Challenges and Criticisms of Communism

While communism has undergone significant transformations over time, it continues to face contemporary challenges and criticisms. This chapter explores the current issues and debates surrounding communism in the modern world. By examining these challenges and criticisms, we can gain a comprehensive understanding of the complexities and limitations of communist ideologies and their practical implementation.

1. Economic Challenges:

One of the primary criticisms of communism relates to its economic model. This section discusses the challenges associated with centrally planned economies and the absence of market mechanisms. We explore issues such as inefficiency, lack of innovation, and the difficulty of resource allocation. We also discuss the impact of globalization and the changing global economic landscape on communist economies.

2. Political Authoritarianism:

Communist regimes have often been associated with political authoritarianism, limiting civil liberties, and suppressing dissent. This section examines the challenges posed by the concentration of power in the hands of a few, the absence of checks and balances, and the impact on political participation and human rights. We discuss the tension between the revolutionary ideals of communism and the realities of maintaining political control.

3. Lack of Political Pluralism and Democracy:

Another criticism leveled against communism is the lack of political pluralism and democratic institutions. This section explores the challenges of establishing genuine democratic governance within communist systems. We discuss the limitations on political freedoms, the absence of competitive elections, and the impact on citizen participation and representation. We also analyze the potential for political stagnation and lack of accountability in communist regimes.

4. Social and Cultural Challenges:

Communist ideologies often aim to reshape society and culture in line with their principles. However, such attempts can face significant challenges. This section explores issues such as the tension between individual freedoms and collective goals, the impact on cultural diversity, and the suppression of dissenting voices. We also discuss the potential for social inequality and the challenges of promoting social cohesion and unity within a communist framework.

5. Environmental Concerns:

Environmental sustainability and the protection of natural resources have emerged as critical global challenges. This section examines how communist systems have addressed or contributed to these concerns. We discuss issues such as industrialization, resource exploitation, and the potential conflicts between economic development and ecological well-being. We analyze the ability of communist regimes to address environmental challenges and incorporate sustainability into their policies.

6. Legitimacy and Public Support:

The legitimacy of communist regimes and their ability to garner public support is another area of contemporary challenge. This section explores the dynamics of popular legitimacy, examining factors such as social contract, propaganda, coercion, and the role of ideology. We discuss the impact of societal changes, generational shifts, and evolving values on the support or opposition to communist governance.

7. Ideological Reinterpretation and Adaptation:

Communist ideologies have undergone reinterpretation and adaptation in response to contemporary challenges. This section explores how communist parties and movements have modified their principles and strategies to address criticisms and remain relevant. We discuss examples of ideological evolution, including democratic socialism and market-oriented socialism. We analyze the tension between ideological purity and pragmatic adaptation within the communist framework.

Conclusion:

Contemporary challenges and criticisms pose significant hurdles for the evolution and practical implementation of communist ideologies. From economic challenges and political authoritarianism to the lack of political pluralism and environmental concerns, communism faces multifaceted criticisms in the modern world. By critically examining these challenges, we can deepen our understanding of the limitations and complexities of communism as a political and economic system. This analysis informs our assessment of its potential for adaptation, transformation, or alternative approaches in response to the demands and realities of the contemporary global landscape.

Chapter 4: Globalization and International Organizations

Impact of Globalization on World Politics

Globalization has emerged as a defining force in contemporary world politics, reshaping economies, societies, and governance structures. This chapter examines the profound impact of globalization on global politics, exploring its implications for state sovereignty, power dynamics, and the nature of international relations. By analyzing the multifaceted effects of globalization, we can better understand the challenges and opportunities it presents for political systems and actors on the global stage.

1. Economic Globalization and Power Shifts:

The rapid integration of economies through globalization has led to significant power shifts in world politics. This section discusses how economic globalization has influenced the distribution of economic power among states, the rise of multinational corporations, and the increasing interconnectedness of financial systems. We examine the implications of economic interdependence, trade liberalization, and the role of international economic institutions in shaping global power dynamics.

2. Transnational Movements and Non-State Actors:

Globalization has facilitated the emergence of transnational movements and non-state actors as influential players in world politics. This section explores the rise of civil society organizations, transnational advocacy networks, and social movements that transcend national boundaries. We discuss how these actors mobilize around issues such as human rights, environmental protection, and social justice, challenging traditional state-centric approaches to global governance.

3. Communication Technology and Information Flows:

The advancements in communication technology have revolutionized information flows and connectivity, profoundly impacting global politics. This section examines the role of digital media, social networks, and internet-based platforms in shaping political discourse, facilitating mobilization, and challenging traditional power structures. We discuss the implications of the digital divide, cyber warfare, and the use of technology in promoting democratic values or enabling authoritarian control.

4. Cultural Exchange and Identity Politics:

Globalization has facilitated cultural exchange and intensified debates around identity politics. This section explores the impact of cultural globalization on national identities, cultural diversity, and the rise of global popular culture. We discuss the challenges posed by cultural homogenization, cultural imperialism, and the potential for intercultural dialogue and understanding as a catalyst for peaceful coexistence in a globalized world.

5. Global Challenges and Collective Action:

Globalization has brought forth a range of transnational challenges that require collective action and international cooperation. This section examines global issues such as climate change, terrorism, pandemics, and migration, highlighting how globalization both exacerbates and enables responses to these challenges. We discuss the role of international organizations, multilateral diplomacy, and global governance mechanisms in addressing these complex problems.

6. Power and Resistance in a Globalized World:

Globalization has generated both winners and losers, leading to power imbalances and resistance from various actors. This section explores the dynamics of power in a globalized world, analyzing how states, corporations, and non-state actors navigate and contest these power structures. We discuss the challenges posed by asymmetrical power relations, the role of regionalism, and the potential for alternative visions of globalization.

7. Sovereignty and Global Governance:

The sovereignty of nation-states has been challenged by the forces of globalization and the increasing interdependence of global issues. This section examines debates surrounding state sovereignty, national autonomy, and the evolving nature of global governance. We discuss the tension between national interests and collective global responsibilities, as well as the potential for innovative governance models that bridge the global-local divide.

Conclusion:

The impact of globalization on world politics is far-reaching and complex, influencing state behavior, power dynamics, and the nature of international relations. Economic globalization, transnational movements, technological advancements, and cultural exchange all shape the global political landscape. Understanding the implications of globalization is crucial for policymakers, scholars, and citizens alike as they navigate the opportunities and challenges presented by an interconnected and interdependent world. By critically examining the impact of globalization on world politics, we can better comprehend the complexities of contemporary global governance and explore avenues for addressing global challenges collectively.

Role and Significance of International Organizations

International organizations play a pivotal role in shaping global politics and facilitating cooperation among nations in the era of globalization. This chapter examines the diverse functions, structures, and significance of international organizations in addressing global challenges, promoting peace and security, fostering economic development, and advancing international cooperation. By analyzing the role of international organizations, we can better understand their impact on the global stage and their potential for effective global governance.

1. Functions of International Organizations:

This section explores the various functions performed by international organizations. We discuss their roles in providing platforms for dialogue and negotiation, mediating conflicts, promoting human rights and sustainable development, coordinating global responses to crises, and facilitating cooperation in areas such as trade, health, and the environment. We examine how international organizations contribute to global governance, acting as intermediaries between states and providing mechanisms for collective decision-making.

2. Types and Structures of International Organizations:

International organizations vary in their mandates, membership, and organizational structures. This section examines the different types of international organizations, including intergovernmental organizations (IGOs) such as the United Nations (UN), regional organizations, and non-governmental organizations (NGOs). We discuss their diverse structures, decision-making processes, and membership criteria, highlighting the advantages and challenges associated with each type.

3. The United Nations and its Specialized Agencies:

The United Nations is the most prominent and comprehensive intergovernmental organization. This section delves into the history, structure, and functions of the UN, emphasizing its role in maintaining international peace and security, promoting human rights, fostering development, and coordinating global cooperation. We also explore the roles and significance of UN specialized agencies, such as the World Health Organization (WHO) and the United Nations Educational, Scientific and Cultural Organization (UNESCO).

4. Regional Organizations and Integration:

Regional organizations have gained prominence in the era of globalization. This section examines the roles and significance of regional organizations, such as the European Union (EU), the African Union (AU), and the Association of Southeast Asian Nations (ASEAN). We discuss their efforts in promoting regional integration, addressing regional challenges, and enhancing cooperation among member states. We analyze the strengths and limitations of regional organizations in complementing global governance efforts.

5. Economic Organizations and Development:

Economic organizations play a vital role in facilitating global economic cooperation and development. This section focuses on international economic institutions such as the International Monetary Fund (IMF), the World Bank, and the World Trade Organization (WTO). We discuss their mandates, functions, and impact on global economic governance, including their roles in promoting financial stability, poverty reduction, and trade liberalization. We also examine debates and criticisms surrounding their effectiveness and inclusivity.

6. Humanitarian and Human Rights Organizations:

Humanitarian and human rights organizations have become integral players in addressing global crises and advocating for human rights. This section explores the roles and significance of organizations such as the International Committee of the Red Cross (ICRC), Amnesty International, and Human Rights Watch. We discuss their efforts in providing humanitarian assistance, monitoring human rights violations, and advocating for justice and accountability. We also analyze the challenges they face in a complex and politically sensitive global landscape.

7. Challenges and Reforms:

International organizations face a range of challenges in fulfilling their mandates and adapting to changing global dynamics. This section examines challenges such as power imbalances, geopolitical tensions, resource constraints, and issues of accountability and transparency. We discuss ongoing debates and proposed reforms aimed at enhancing the effectiveness, legitimacy, and inclusivity of international organizations. We also explore the potential for innovation and cooperation between international organizations and non-state actors in addressing global challenges.

Conclusion:

International organizations play a crucial role in addressing global challenges, fostering cooperation, and promoting collective decision-making in an interconnected world. From peace and security to economic development and human rights, these organizations have a significant impact on the global stage. However, they also face inherent challenges and calls for reform. Understanding the roles, structures, and significance of international organizations is essential for comprehending the dynamics of global governance and exploring avenues for effective and inclusive global cooperation.

Challenges and Opportunities in a Globalized World

Globalization has transformed the world into an interconnected and interdependent system, presenting both challenges and opportunities for nations, societies, and individuals. This chapter explores the complex dynamics of a globalized world, examining the key challenges and opportunities that arise from increased interconnectivity. By analyzing these factors, we can better understand the implications for global politics, governance, and cooperation, as well as the role of international organizations in addressing these challenges and harnessing the opportunities.

1. Economic Challenges and Opportunities:

Globalization has generated both economic challenges and opportunities for nations. This section examines the challenges of economic inequality, trade imbalances, and financial instability in a globalized economy. It also explores the opportunities presented by increased access to markets, technological advancements, and the potential for economic growth through international trade and investment. We discuss the role of international organizations in promoting economic stability, reducing poverty, and addressing economic disparities.

2. Environmental Challenges and Opportunities:

The process of globalization has significantly impacted the environment, presenting both challenges and opportunities for sustainable development. This section discusses the challenges of climate change, resource depletion, and environmental degradation resulting from increased global economic activities. It explores the opportunities for international cooperation, environmental governance, and the adoption of sustainable practices to mitigate these challenges. We examine the role of international organizations in facilitating environmental agreements, promoting conservation, and addressing transboundary environmental issues.

3. Social and Cultural Challenges and Opportunities:

Globalization has led to the diffusion of cultures, ideas, and values, impacting social dynamics and cultural identities. This section explores the challenges of cultural homogenization, cultural clashes, and the erosion of local traditions and values in a globalized world. It also examines the opportunities for cultural exchange, intercultural dialogue, and the preservation of cultural diversity. We discuss the role of international organizations in promoting cultural understanding, protecting cultural heritage, and facilitating cross-cultural cooperation.

4. Technological Challenges and Opportunities:

Technological advancements and digital connectivity have revolutionized global interactions, presenting both challenges and opportunities. This section examines the challenges of cybersecurity threats, digital divide, and the impact of automation on employment in a globalized digital economy. It explores the opportunities for innovation, knowledge sharing, and technological advancements that can enhance productivity and improve quality of life. We discuss the role of international organizations in addressing technological challenges, setting standards, and promoting digital inclusion.

5. Governance Challenges and Opportunities:

Globalization has redefined traditional notions of governance, raising challenges and opportunities for effective global governance. This section discusses the challenges of power imbalances, global governance gaps, and the limitations of state-centric approaches in a globalized world. It explores the opportunities for multilateralism, inclusive governance, and the role of international organizations in fostering cooperation and addressing global challenges. We analyze efforts to reform global governance structures and enhance the legitimacy and effectiveness of international organizations.

6. Security Challenges and Opportunities:

Globalization has reshaped the security landscape, introducing new challenges and opportunities for international security. This section examines the challenges of transnational threats such as terrorism, organized crime, and cyber warfare. It explores the opportunities for collective security, cooperation in peacekeeping, and the role of international organizations in conflict prevention and resolution. We discuss efforts to enhance global security architecture and address emerging security challenges through international collaboration.

7. Ethical and Moral Challenges:

Globalization raises ethical and moral questions regarding the responsibilities of individuals, nations, and international organizations. This section explores the challenges of ethical dilemmas, human rights violations, and the potential for exploitation in a globalized world. It discusses the opportunities for promoting ethical behavior, human rights protection, and responsible governance. We examine the role of international organizations in upholding ethical standards, promoting accountability, and addressing global ethical challenges.

Conclusion:

Globalization presents a complex web of challenges and opportunities in various spheres of human activity.

International organizations play a crucial role in addressing these challenges, harnessing opportunities, and fostering cooperation. By understanding the multifaceted nature of globalization, we can work towards shaping a globalized world that promotes sustainable development, inclusivity, and the well-being of all individuals and societies.

Sovereignty and Global Governance

The process of globalization has reshaped traditional notions of sovereignty and raised important questions about the relationship between national autonomy and global governance. This chapter examines the challenges and opportunities that arise in navigating the tension between sovereignty and the need for effective global governance. By analyzing the dynamics of sovereignty in a globalized world, as well as the role of international organizations, we can gain insights into how global governance structures can accommodate and address these complexities.

1. Understanding Sovereignty:

This section provides an overview of the concept of sovereignty and its historical evolution. We discuss the traditional understanding of sovereignty as state-centric and explore how globalization has challenged this notion. We examine the components of sovereignty, including territorial integrity, political independence, and decision-making authority. Furthermore, we analyze the impact of globalization on the exercise of sovereignty and the emergence of new actors and factors that influence it.

2. Global Governance and the Erosion of Sovereignty:

Global governance refers to the collective efforts of states and international organizations to address global challenges and manage common affairs. This section explores how globalization has led to the erosion of sovereignty in certain areas. We discuss the increasing interdependence of states, the proliferation of international norms and agreements, and the transfer of authority to supranational bodies. We examine the challenges posed by the need for global governance and the potential tension between national sovereignty and international cooperation.

3. The Role of International Organizations in Global Governance:

International organizations play a significant role in global governance by providing platforms for cooperation, establishing norms, and facilitating collective decision-making. This section examines how international organizations navigate the complexities of sovereignty while promoting global cooperation. We discuss their role in setting standards, facilitating negotiations, and implementing agreements in areas such as trade, security, human rights, and the environment. We analyze the challenges they face in striking a balance between respecting sovereignty and achieving effective global governance.

4. The Sovereignty-Intervention Dilemma:

One of the key challenges in global governance is the tension between sovereignty and the responsibility to protect and promote human rights. This section explores the sovereignty-intervention dilemma, examining debates surrounding humanitarian interventions, the responsibility to protect (R2P), and the limits of state sovereignty. We discuss cases where the international community has grappled with intervention decisions, weighing the principles of sovereignty and human rights. We also examine the role of international organizations in facilitating dialogue and mediating disputes in this context.

5. Sovereignty and Economic Globalization:

Economic globalization presents challenges and opportunities for state sovereignty. This section explores how economic interdependence impacts sovereignty, particularly in the context of trade agreements, investment flows, and financial regulations. We discuss the role of international organizations in shaping global economic governance and the challenges faced in reconciling national economic policies with global economic integration. We examine debates surrounding the impact of trade agreements on sovereignty, including issues of regulatory harmonization and investor-state dispute settlement.

6. Regionalism and Sovereignty:

Regional integration initiatives present unique dynamics in the context of sovereignty. This section examines regional organizations and the challenges and opportunities they pose to national sovereignty. We discuss the experiences of regional blocs such as the European Union (EU), the African Union (AU), and the Association of Southeast Asian Nations (ASEAN). We analyze the extent to which regional integration impacts national sovereignty, considering the delegation of authority, the pooling of resources, and the harmonization of policies within regional frameworks.

7. Sovereignty in the Digital Age:

The advent of digital technologies has further complicated the sovereignty debate. This section explores the challenges posed by cyberspace, data privacy, and the transnational flow of information. We examine how states and international organizations navigate the tension between national control and the open nature of the internet. We discuss the role of international organizations in promoting global norms and regulations in cyberspace and addressing issues of sovereignty and jurisdiction in the digital age.

Conclusion:

The tension between sovereignty and global governance is a central issue in the era of globalization. While sovereignty remains a fundamental principle, the complexities of global challenges require cooperation and collective action. International organizations play a crucial role in balancing the demands of sovereignty and global governance, facilitating dialogue, and forging agreements among nations. By understanding these dynamics, we can navigate the challenges of sovereignty in a globalized world and work towards more effective and inclusive global governance structures.

Chapter 5: Nationalism and Populism
Rise of Nationalist and Populist Movements

The rise of nationalist and populist movements has had a significant impact on global politics in recent years. This chapter delves into the origins, drivers, and consequences of these movements. By examining their rise in different regions and analyzing their ideologies and strategies, we can gain a comprehensive understanding of the factors contributing to their popularity and the implications they have for domestic and international affairs.

1. Understanding Nationalism and Populism:

This section provides a foundational understanding of nationalism and populism. We explore the historical context and ideological underpinnings of these movements, examining their core principles and objectives. We distinguish between civic and ethnic nationalism, as well as left-wing and right-wing populism, highlighting the diverse manifestations and motivations within these broader categories.

2. Socioeconomic Factors and Discontent:

This section delves into the socioeconomic factors that contribute to the rise of nationalist and populist movements. We analyze the impact of economic inequality, globalization, and technological advancements on societal dynamics. We explore how these factors can lead to a sense of marginalization, anxiety, and loss of identity among certain segments of the population, which nationalist and populist leaders often exploit.

3. Cultural Identity and Migration:

The issue of cultural identity and immigration plays a significant role in fueling nationalist and populist movements. This section examines the relationship between identity politics, cultural anxieties, and the perception of threat posed by immigration. We analyze the ways in which nationalist and populist leaders use narratives of cultural preservation, national heritage, and border control to appeal to their supporters.

4. Political Factors and Anti-Establishment Sentiment:

The rise of nationalist and populist movements is closely linked to a widespread disillusionment with mainstream political establishments. This section explores the political factors that contribute to their popularity, such as dissatisfaction with traditional political parties, perceived corruption, and a desire for alternative leadership. We examine the strategies employed by nationalist and populist leaders to position themselves as anti-establishment figures.

5. Technological Influence and Disinformation:

The advent of digital technologies and social media platforms has had a profound impact on the rise of nationalist and populist movements. This section examines how these movements utilize online platforms to disseminate their messages, mobilize supporters, and spread disinformation. We analyze the role of echo chambers, filter bubbles, and targeted advertising in shaping public opinion and amplifying nationalist and populist narratives.

6. Regional Case Studies:

This section provides a comparative analysis of nationalist and populist movements in different regions. We examine case studies from various parts of the world, such as Europe, North America, Asia, and Latin America, to highlight the regional variations in nationalist and populist ideologies, strategies, and electoral success. We explore the factors that contribute to their rise in each context, including historical legacies, socioeconomic conditions, and geopolitical dynamics.

7. Impact on Democracy and International Relations:

The rise of nationalist and populist movements has significant implications for democratic governance and international relations. This section examines the challenges these movements pose to democratic institutions, including the erosion of checks and balances, attacks on the rule of law, and the restriction of civil liberties. We also analyze the impact of nationalist and populist ideologies on international relations, including the potential for increased nationalism, protectionism, and the reconfiguration of global alliances.

Conclusion:

The rise of nationalist and populist movements reflects deep-seated societal tensions and challenges prevailing political norms. Understanding the drivers and consequences of these movements is crucial for navigating the complex landscape of global politics. By analyzing the socioeconomic, cultural, political, and technological factors that contribute to their rise, we can foster informed dialogue and develop strategies to address the underlying grievances and ensure a more inclusive and resilient democratic framework.

Causes and Consequences of Nationalism

Nationalism has been a powerful force in shaping societies and political landscapes throughout history. This chapter explores the causes and consequences of nationalism, with a focus on its contemporary manifestations. By examining the historical roots, underlying drivers, and implications of nationalism, we can gain insights into its impact on domestic politics, international relations, and the broader global order.

1. Understanding Nationalism:

This section provides a comprehensive understanding of nationalism as a political ideology and social phenomenon. We explore its historical development, from its origins in the nation-state-building processes of the 19th century to its relevance in the present day. We delve into the conceptual foundations of nationalism, including the ideas of cultural identity, shared history, and collective aspirations.

2. Historical Context and Origins:

This section delves into the historical context that gave rise to nationalism. We explore how factors such as colonialism, industrialization, and revolutions contributed to the emergence of nationalist sentiments. We analyze case studies from different regions to highlight the specific historical events and dynamics that fueled nationalist movements, such as the unification of Italy and Germany or the decolonization movements in Africa and Asia.

3. Cultural and Identity Factors:

Cultural and identity factors play a significant role in the development of nationalism. This section examines how language, religion, ethnicity, and cultural traditions shape national identities. We explore how nationalist movements often rely on cultural symbols, historical narratives, and shared values to foster a sense of belonging and mobilize support. We also discuss the tensions between inclusive civic nationalism and exclusive ethnic nationalism.

4. Socioeconomic Factors and Grievances:

Socioeconomic factors and grievances can contribute to the rise of nationalist sentiments. This section analyzes how economic inequality, perceived loss of jobs or resources, and feelings of marginalization can fuel nationalist movements. We explore how nationalist leaders often capitalize on these grievances and offer promises of economic protectionism, redistribution, or the restoration of past glories to gain support.

5. Political Factors and Leadership:

Political factors, such as weak governance, political instability, or a perceived lack of representation, can create fertile ground for nationalist movements to thrive. This section examines how nationalist leaders often position themselves as champions of the people against corrupt elites or foreign influences. We explore their strategies for consolidating power, manipulating public sentiment, and leveraging populist rhetoric to maintain support.

6. Nationalism and International Relations:

The consequences of nationalism extend beyond domestic politics. This section analyzes the impact of nationalism on international relations, including its role in shaping foreign policy, bilateral relations, and regional dynamics. We discuss how nationalist movements can lead to tensions, conflicts, or even the redrawing of borders. We also explore the interplay between nationalism and globalization, considering the tensions between national sovereignty and international cooperation.

7. Consequences and Challenges:

The consequences of nationalism are multifaceted and can have both positive and negative outcomes. This section examines the potential benefits, such as fostering a sense of unity, promoting national pride, or driving economic development. However, we also critically analyze the challenges and negative consequences associated with nationalism, such as the potential for exclusionary policies, discrimination against minority groups, or the erosion of democratic institutions.

Conclusion:

Nationalism continues to shape political landscapes and international relations in the contemporary world. By understanding its causes and consequences, we can navigate the complexities of nationalism and its impact on societies, governance, and global cooperation. It is crucial to strike a balance between the legitimate aspirations for self-determination and identity preservation while upholding the principles of inclusivity, respect for diversity, and cooperation among nations.

The rise of populism has sparked debates about its compatibility with democratic principles and institutions. This chapter examines the complex relationship between populism and democracy, exploring the origins, characteristics, and implications of populist movements within democratic contexts. By analyzing the dynamics between populism and democracy, we can gain insights into the challenges and potential consequences for democratic governance.

1. Understanding Populism:

This section provides a comprehensive understanding of populism as a political ideology and phenomenon. We delve into its historical roots and ideological foundations, examining how populism differentiates itself from other political ideologies. We discuss the core elements of populism, including the people-centric rhetoric, anti-elitism, and the notion of a homogeneous "will of the people."

2. The Democratic Ideal:

This section explores the foundational principles of democracy and its core values, such as popular sovereignty, political equality, and protection of individual rights. We discuss the mechanisms of democratic governance, including free and fair elections, rule of law, separation of powers, and protection of civil liberties. We highlight the importance of democratic institutions and their role in safeguarding democratic processes.

3. Populism as a Democratic Response:

This section examines the reasons behind the rise of populism within democratic systems. We explore how populist movements often emerge in response to perceived failures or deficiencies in democratic governance. We analyze the discontent and grievances that drive individuals to support populist leaders and parties, such as socioeconomic inequalities, political corruption, or a sense of marginalization.

4. Populism and Democratic Institutions:

This section delves into the relationship between populism and democratic institutions. We analyze how populist leaders may challenge or undermine democratic institutions, including the executive, legislative, and judicial branches. We discuss the potential consequences of populist attacks on the media, civil society organizations, and other checks and balances essential for a functioning democracy.

5. Populist Leadership and Political Style:

This section examines the role of populist leaders within democratic systems. We explore their charismatic appeal, communication strategies, and direct engagement with their supporters. We discuss the ways in which populist leaders often adopt confrontational rhetoric, polarizing narratives, and appeal to emotions rather than evidence-based policy-making.

6. Challenges to Liberal Democracy:

This section analyzes the challenges posed by populism to liberal democracy. We examine how populist movements may promote illiberal practices, such as restrictions on individual rights, attacks on minority groups, or the erosion of the rule of law. We discuss the potential for populism to undermine democratic norms, including respect for diversity, tolerance, and pluralism.

7. Balancing Populist Demands and Democratic Values:

This section explores the complexities of balancing populism and democratic values. We discuss the importance of addressing the underlying grievances that fuel populism while upholding the fundamental principles of democracy. We examine strategies for fostering inclusive political dialogue, strengthening democratic institutions, and promoting social and economic policies that address the concerns of marginalized populations.

8. Populism and Democratic Renewal:

This section highlights the potential for populism to serve as a catalyst for democratic renewal. We explore how the emergence of populist movements can stimulate public debate, political engagement, and a reevaluation of democratic practices. We discuss the importance of responsive and accountable governance, addressing socioeconomic inequalities, and restoring trust in democratic institutions.

Conclusion:

The relationship between populism and democracy is complex and multifaceted. While populism can be seen as a response to perceived democratic deficits, it also poses challenges to democratic values and institutions. Understanding the dynamics between populism and democracy is crucial for safeguarding the principles of democratic governance, fostering inclusive political participation, and addressing the underlying social and economic concerns that fuel populist sentiments. It is essential to strive for a balanced approach that upholds democratic principles while addressing the legitimate grievances of citizens.

Nationalism and populism have significant implications for international relations, shaping the interactions between states, the dynamics of global governance, and the pursuit of collective solutions to global challenges. This chapter explores the impact of nationalism and populism on international relations, examining how these ideologies influence foreign policy, international cooperation, and the global order.

1. Nationalism and Foreign Policy:

This section explores how nationalism and populism influence a state's foreign policy decisions. We examine how nationalist sentiments can shape a country's approach to issues such as territorial disputes, trade policies, migration, and alliances. We discuss the potential for nationalist ideologies to prioritize national interests over international cooperation and the challenges this poses for diplomacy and multilateralism.

2. Populist Movements and Globalization:

This section analyzes the relationship between populism and globalization, exploring how populist movements respond to the challenges and opportunities presented by an interconnected world. We discuss the ways in which populist leaders may promote protectionist trade policies, advocate for restrictions on immigration, or challenge international agreements and institutions. We also examine the potential consequences of such policies on global economic stability and cooperation.

3. Nationalism, Populism, and International Organizations:

This section examines the implications of nationalism and populism for international organizations. We discuss the tensions that arise when nationalist governments question the authority or effectiveness of global governance institutions, such as the United Nations, the World Trade Organization, or regional organizations. We explore how nationalist and populist movements may prioritize sovereignty over international cooperation, impacting the functioning and legitimacy of these organizations.

4. Nationalism, Populism, and Security:

This section explores the implications of nationalism and populism for security dynamics at the global level. We analyze how nationalist ideologies can influence perceptions of national security threats, the prioritization of defense spending, and the willingness to engage in military interventions. We discuss the potential for nationalist rhetoric to exacerbate tensions between states, leading to increased competition and a potential erosion of collective security mechanisms.

5. Nationalism, Populism, and Global Challenges:

This section examines how nationalism and populism shape responses to global challenges, such as climate change, pandemics, or migration. We discuss how these ideologies can influence a state's willingness to engage in international cooperation, share the burden of addressing global problems, and contribute to global governance mechanisms. We explore the potential for nationalist and populist movements to hinder collective action and the implications for addressing transnational issues.

6. Nationalism, Populism, and International Alliances:

This section focuses on the impact of nationalism and populism on international alliances and partnerships. We examine how nationalist and populist leaders may challenge or question existing alliances, renegotiate international agreements, or pursue unilateral policies. We discuss the potential consequences for collective defense, regional stability, and the broader network of international alliances.

7. Balancing National Interests and Global Cooperation:

This section explores the challenges of balancing national interests with the imperative for international cooperation. We discuss the importance of inclusive and constructive dialogue between nationalist and populist movements and the international community. We examine strategies for finding common ground, building trust, and promoting shared values to address global challenges while respecting the concerns and aspirations of nation-states.

Conclusion:

Nationalism and populism have far-reaching implications for international relations. Understanding how these ideologies shape foreign policy decisions, global governance structures, and responses to global challenges is essential for navigating the complexities of the contemporary international system. It is crucial to seek a balance between national interests and international cooperation, fostering dialogue, and promoting multilateral approaches to address global issues effectively while respecting the diverse perspectives and aspirations of nations in an interconnected world.

Chapter 6: Political Ideologies and Movements
Liberalism: Origins, Principles, and Variations

Liberalism is one of the most influential political ideologies that emerged in the modern era. This chapter explores the origins, key principles, and variations of liberalism. We delve into its historical context, examine its core tenets, and analyze how it has evolved and adapted in different cultural and political contexts.

1. Historical Origins of Liberalism:

This section delves into the historical origins of liberalism, tracing its development from the Enlightenment period to the present day. We explore the intellectual roots of liberalism in thinkers such as John Locke, Adam Smith, and John Stuart Mill, highlighting their contributions to liberal thought. We discuss how historical events and societal transformations shaped the emergence of liberalism as a response to challenges of the time.

2. Key Principles of Liberalism:

This section examines the fundamental principles that underpin liberalism. We discuss concepts such as individual liberty, limited government, the rule of law, and constitutionalism. We explore how liberalism emphasizes the protection of individual rights and freedoms, the importance of a market-based economy, and the belief in the value of pluralism and tolerance.

3. Liberalism and Individual Rights:

This section focuses on the liberal emphasis on individual rights and freedoms. We discuss the concept of natural rights, including civil liberties such as freedom of speech, religion, and assembly. We explore the idea of equality of opportunity, the right to private property, and the role of the state in protecting and safeguarding individual rights.

4. Economic Liberalism:

This section explores the economic dimension of liberalism, commonly known as economic liberalism or classical liberalism. We discuss the principles of free markets, limited government intervention, and the importance of property rights. We examine the impact of economic liberalism on wealth creation, economic growth, and the relationship between the state and the market.

5. Variations of Liberalism:

This section analyzes the variations and adaptations of liberalism across different regions and historical periods. We discuss how liberalism has taken different forms, such as social liberalism, neoliberalism, and libertarianism. We examine the differences in emphasis and policy preferences within the liberal tradition, exploring debates around the role of the state in promoting social justice, the balance between individual rights and collective responsibilities, and the scope of government intervention.

6. Liberalism and Democracy:

This section explores the relationship between liberalism and democracy. We discuss how liberalism's commitment to individual rights and freedoms intersects with democratic principles such as popular sovereignty, political participation, and the protection of minority rights. We examine the challenges and tensions that can arise between liberal and democratic ideals, particularly in contexts where illiberal democracy or populist movements emerge.

7. Liberalism in Practice:

This section examines examples of liberalism in practice, highlighting countries or regions where liberal ideas have had a significant influence on governance and policy-making. We explore case studies that illustrate the implementation of liberal principles, including the development of liberal democracies, the expansion of civil liberties, and the promotion of free-market economies.

8. Criticisms and Challenges to Liberalism:

This section critically examines the criticisms and challenges faced by liberalism. We discuss arguments from various ideological perspectives, such as communitarianism, feminism, and postcolonialism, questioning the liberal emphasis on individualism, market-driven solutions, and the potential for unequal outcomes. We explore debates around the limits of liberalism in addressing social inequalities, environmental concerns, and cultural diversity.

Conclusion:

Liberalism, with its emphasis on individual rights, limited government, and free markets, has shaped political and economic systems worldwide. By understanding its historical origins, key principles, variations, and challenges, we gain insights into the strengths and limitations of liberal thought. Acknowledging the diversity of liberal perspectives and engaging in critical dialogue about its application in different contexts is essential for promoting an inclusive and responsive political order that balances individual freedoms with the collective well-being of society.

Conservatism is a political ideology that emphasizes the preservation of traditional values, institutions, and social order. This chapter explores the origins, key principles, and variations of conservatism. We delve into its historical context, examine its core tenets, and analyze how it has evolved and adapted in different cultural and political contexts.

1. Historical Origins of Conservatism:

This section delves into the historical origins of conservatism, tracing its development from the reaction to the French Revolution to the present day. We explore the intellectual roots of conservatism in thinkers such as Edmund Burke, Joseph de Maistre, and Michael Oakeshott, highlighting their contributions to conservative thought. We discuss how historical events and societal transformations shaped the emergence of conservatism as a response to challenges of the time.

2. Key Principles of Conservatism:

This section examines the fundamental principles that underpin conservatism. We discuss concepts such as tradition, hierarchy, authority, and organic society. We explore how conservatism emphasizes the importance of preserving established institutions, customs, and cultural norms as the foundation of social order and stability. We analyze the conservative belief in the value of gradual change, the skepticism toward radical social engineering, and the emphasis on individual responsibility and self-reliance.

3. Conservatism and Traditional Values:

This section focuses on the conservative emphasis on traditional values and morality. We discuss how conservatism upholds traditional social, religious, and cultural norms as essential for maintaining social cohesion and stability. We explore the conservative perspective on family, community, and the role of religion in shaping societal values. We also examine how conservatism responds to social change and the challenges posed by cultural diversity and globalization.

4. Economic Conservatism:

This section explores the economic dimension of conservatism, commonly known as economic conservatism or fiscal conservatism. We discuss the principles of limited government intervention, free markets, and the importance of private property rights. We examine the conservative belief in the value of individual initiative, entrepreneurship, and the promotion of economic growth. We also analyze debates within conservatism regarding the role of the state in addressing social inequalities and providing a safety net.

5. Variations of Conservatism:

This section analyzes the variations and adaptations of conservatism across different regions and historical periods. We discuss how conservatism has taken different forms, such as traditional conservatism, neoconservatism, and libertarian conservatism. We examine the differences in emphasis and policy preferences within the conservative tradition, exploring debates around social welfare, environmental stewardship, and the balance between individual liberties and societal order.

6. Conservatism and Democracy:

This section explores the relationship between conservatism and democracy. We discuss how conservatism's emphasis on tradition, hierarchy, and authority intersects with democratic principles such as popular sovereignty and political participation. We examine the tensions and challenges that can arise between conservative values and democratic processes, particularly in contexts where conservatism clashes with liberal democratic ideals or faces criticism for its potential to perpetuate inequalities.

7. Conservatism in Practice:

This section examines examples of conservatism in practice, highlighting countries or regions where conservative ideas have had a significant influence on governance and policy-making. We explore case studies that illustrate the implementation of conservative principles, including the defense of traditional institutions, the promotion of social cohesion, and the pursuit of economic stability.

8. Criticisms and Challenges to Conservatism:

This section critically examines the criticisms and challenges faced by conservatism. We discuss arguments from various ideological perspectives, such as liberalism, socialism, and feminism, questioning the conservative emphasis on hierarchy, inequality, and the potential limitations on individual freedoms. We explore debates around the adaptability of conservative thought in addressing social justice concerns, environmental sustainability, and changing societal values.

Conclusion:

Conservatism, with its emphasis on traditional values, social order, and limited government intervention, has played a significant role in shaping political landscapes around the world. By understanding its historical roots, key principles, variations, and challenges, we gain valuable

insights into the complex dynamics of conservative thought
and its impact on societies.

Socialism: Equality, Redistribution, and Public Ownership

Socialism is a political ideology rooted in the pursuit of social and economic equality. This chapter explores the origins, key principles, and variations of socialism. We delve into its historical context, examine its core tenets, and analyze how it has evolved and adapted in different cultural and political contexts.

1. Historical Origins of Socialism:

This section provides an overview of the historical origins of socialism, tracing its development from early utopian visions to the emergence of socialist movements and parties. We explore the intellectual roots of socialism in thinkers such as Karl Marx, Friedrich Engels, and Robert Owen, highlighting their contributions to socialist thought. We discuss the impact of industrialization, class struggles, and socioeconomic inequalities on the rise of socialist ideologies.

2. Key Principles of Socialism:

This section examines the fundamental principles that underpin socialism. We discuss concepts such as economic equality, social justice, and collective ownership of resources and means of production. We explore how socialism seeks to address the inherent contradictions and injustices of capitalism through the redistribution of wealth, the provision of social welfare, and the promotion of worker's rights. We analyze the socialist critique of private property and its vision for a more equitable society.

3. Economic Models of Socialism:

This section explores different economic models associated with socialism. We discuss the concepts of central planning, state ownership, and public control over key industries and resources. We examine variations within socialism, such as democratic socialism, market socialism, and planned economies. We analyze the advantages and challenges of implementing different economic models of socialism, including considerations of efficiency, innovation, and individual freedoms.

4. Socialism and Equality:

This section focuses on the socialist pursuit of equality. We discuss how socialism seeks to address socioeconomic disparities, eliminate poverty, and ensure access to essential resources and services for all members of society. We explore the concept of distributive justice and the role of the state in redistributing wealth and reducing inequalities. We also analyze debates within socialism regarding the balance between equality and individual incentives.

5. Socialism and Social Welfare:

This section examines the socialist perspective on social welfare and the provision of public goods and services. We discuss the role of the state in guaranteeing healthcare, education, housing, and other essential needs. We explore the socialist critique of market-based approaches to social welfare and the arguments for collective responsibility and solidarity. We also analyze challenges and trade-offs in funding and implementing comprehensive social welfare programs.

6. Variations of Socialism:

This section analyzes the variations and adaptations of socialism across different regions and historical periods. We discuss how socialism has taken different forms, such as democratic socialism, Marxist-Leninism, and social democracy. We examine the differences in emphasis and policy preferences within the socialist tradition, including debates around the role of the state, political participation, and the balance between economic planning and market mechanisms.

7. Socialism and Democracy:

This section explores the relationship between socialism and democracy. We discuss how socialism seeks to combine economic equality with political participation and democratic decision-making. We examine the challenges and tensions that can arise when implementing socialist ideals within democratic frameworks, including debates around individual freedoms, political pluralism, and the role of civil society.

8. Socialism in Practice:

This section examines examples of socialism in practice, highlighting countries or regions where socialist ideas have had a significant influence on governance and policy-making. We explore case studies that illustrate the implementation of socialist principles, including the nationalization of industries, the establishment of welfare states, and experiments with participatory democracy. We analyze the successes, failures, and challenges faced by socialist governments and movements.

9. Criticisms and Challenges to Socialism:

This section critically examines the criticisms and challenges faced by socialism. We explore critiques from different ideological perspectives, including concerns about economic efficiency, individual liberties, and the role of markets. We also discuss challenges related to political repression, lack of innovation, and the potential for authoritarianism in some socialist systems. We address the debate surrounding the viability and sustainability of socialist models in the face of global economic interdependencies.

Conclusion:

In the conclusion, we summarize the key principles, variations, and challenges of socialism. We reflect on the historical significance and ongoing relevance of socialist thought and its impact on political, economic, and social systems. We also explore the potential for dialogue and synthesis between socialist ideals and other political ideologies in addressing contemporary challenges and envisioning alternative futures.

In addition to liberalism, conservatism, and socialism, there are numerous other ideological perspectives that have shaped political landscapes and influenced societies around the world. This chapter explores some of these alternative ideologies, examining their origins, core principles, and their impact on politics, governance, and social movements. By understanding these diverse perspectives, we gain a more comprehensive understanding of the complex tapestry of political ideologies and their role in shaping societies.

1. Anarchism:

This section explores the ideology of anarchism, which advocates for the abolition of hierarchical authority and the establishment of a stateless society. We examine the historical roots of anarchism, from thinkers such as Pierre-Joseph Proudhon and Mikhail Bakunin to contemporary anarchist movements. We discuss the principles of voluntary association, direct democracy, and non-violent resistance central to anarchism, as well as the challenges and criticisms it has faced.

2. Feminism:

This section delves into the ideology of feminism, which seeks to challenge and transform gender inequalities and promote gender justice. We explore the historical development of feminist thought, from first-wave suffragettes to intersectional and postcolonial feminism. We discuss key concepts such as patriarchy, gender equality, and women's rights, and how feminist movements have impacted politics, law, and social norms. We also analyze debates within feminism, including tensions between different feminist perspectives.

3. Environmentalism:

This section focuses on the ideology of environmentalism, which emphasizes the protection of the natural environment and sustainable development. We examine the origins of the environmental movement and key figures such as Rachel Carson and Wangari Maathai. We discuss environmental ethics, conservation, and the challenges posed by climate change and ecological degradation. We also explore the relationship between environmentalism and political action, including green parties and grassroots movements.

4. Nationalism:

This section explores the ideology of nationalism, which emphasizes the primacy of the nation as a political and cultural entity. We discuss the historical development of nationalism, from the era of nation-building to contemporary expressions of ethnic and civic nationalism.

We examine the concepts of national identity, self-determination, and the challenges and controversies associated with nationalism, including its potential for exclusionary and divisive politics.

5. Religious and Ethical Movements:

This section examines the role of religious and ethical movements in shaping political ideologies and social movements. We explore ideologies such as Christian democracy, Islamic fundamentalism, and secular humanism. We discuss how religious and ethical values influence political decision-making, social policies, and moral debates. We also analyze the complexities and tensions that arise when religious and ethical perspectives intersect with secular governance.

6. Postcolonial and Decolonial Thought:

This section focuses on postcolonial and decolonial thought, which critique the legacies of colonialism and imperialism. We examine the works of influential thinkers such as Frantz Fanon and Edward Said, and discuss concepts such as cultural imperialism, subalternity, and the politics of identity. We explore the impact of postcolonial and decolonial thought on anti-colonial movements, cultural production, and the reimagining of history and power dynamics.

7. Technocracy and Transhumanism:

This section explores ideologies that emphasize the role of technology in shaping societies and political systems. We examine technocracy, which advocates for governance by experts, and transhumanism, which envisions the enhancement of human capabilities through technology. We discuss the promises and challenges associated with these ideologies, including questions of elitism, inequality, and ethical implications of technological advancements.

8. Synthesis and Hybrid Ideologies:

This section analyzes the ways in which different ideological perspectives interact and influence one another, leading to the emergence of synthesis and hybrid ideologies. We explore examples such as social democracy, which combines elements of socialism and liberalism, and eco-socialism, which integrates environmental concerns with socialist principles. We discuss the potential for dialogue, synthesis, and adaptation of ideological perspectives in response to contemporary challenges.

Conclusion:

In the conclusion, we reflect on the diversity and complexity of ideological perspectives beyond liberalism, conservatism, and socialism. We highlight the significance of these alternative ideologies in shaping political movements, influencing policy debates, and challenging existing power structures. By understanding these diverse ideological perspectives, we gain a more nuanced understanding of the dynamic nature of political ideologies and their impact on societies.

In this chapter, we examine various case studies of political systems from different regions of the world. By analyzing real-world examples, we gain insights into the complexities, challenges, and successes of different political systems. Through these case studies, we aim to deepen our understanding of how political ideologies and institutions interact with social, economic, and historical contexts.

1. United States of America:

This section focuses on the political system of the United States, highlighting its democratic principles, constitutional framework, and the separation of powers. We examine the historical development of the American political system, including the Founding Fathers' vision and the evolution of democratic governance. We also analyze the key features of the U.S. political system, such as federalism, checks and balances, and the two-party system. We discuss the challenges and debates surrounding issues such as polarization, campaign finance, and voter participation.

2. United Kingdom:

This section explores the political system of the United Kingdom, with a particular focus on the Westminster model of governance. We examine the evolution of the

British political system, including the role of the monarchy, the development of parliamentary democracy, and the influence of political parties. We discuss key institutions and practices such as the Prime Minister, Cabinet, and the House of Commons. We also analyze challenges such as devolution, the relationship with the European Union, and debates on electoral reform.

3. Germany:

This section examines the political system of Germany, highlighting the principles of federalism and proportional representation. We discuss the historical context of the German political system, including the post-World War II division and reunification. We explore the structure and functions of the Bundestag, the Chancellor, and the federal states (Länder). We also analyze the influence of political parties, coalition governments, and the constitutional court. We address challenges such as managing diversity, immigration, and the rise of far-right movements.

4. China:

This section delves into the political system of China, characterized as a socialist one-party state. We examine the historical and ideological foundations of the Chinese political system, including the role of the Communist Party of China.

We discuss the structure and functions of key institutions such as the National People's Congress, the State Council, and the Chinese Communist Party. We analyze the challenges and tensions between political control and economic liberalization, human rights issues, and the evolving role of civil society.

5. India:

This section explores the political system of India, known as the world's largest democracy. We examine the historical development of the Indian political system, including the challenges and successes of post-colonial nation-building. We discuss the structure and functions of key institutions such as the Parliament, the President, and the Supreme Court. We also analyze the diversity of political parties, federalism, and the complex dynamics of caste, religion, and regional identities in Indian politics.

6. South Africa:

This section focuses on the political system of South Africa, highlighting its transition from apartheid to democracy. We examine the historical context of apartheid and the challenges faced in building a multi-racial democracy. We discuss the structure and functions of key institutions such as the Parliament, the President, and the Constitutional Court. We analyze the significance of the

African National Congress, the role of reconciliation and transformation, and ongoing challenges related to inequality, corruption, and social cohesion.

Conclusion:

In the conclusion, we reflect on the diversity and complexity of political systems worldwide as evidenced by the case studies examined in this chapter. We highlight the unique characteristics, challenges, and successes of each political system, emphasizing the importance of context, historical legacy, and the interplay between political institutions and societal factors. By studying these case studies, we gain a deeper understanding of the intricacies of political systems in practice and their implications for governance, democracy, and societal development.

In this chapter, we conduct a comparative analysis of democratic and authoritarian political systems. By examining the strengths, weaknesses, and dynamics of these systems, we aim to understand the contrasting approaches to governance, power distribution, and individual freedoms. Through this comparative analysis, we gain insights into the implications of different political systems on societal development, human rights, and political stability.

1. Understanding Democratic Systems:

This section provides an in-depth exploration of democratic systems, focusing on their key features, principles, and values. We discuss the foundations of democracy, such as popular sovereignty, rule of law, and protection of individual rights. We examine the different models of democracy, including presidential and parliamentary systems, and highlight examples from around the world. We also analyze the challenges and complexities associated with democratic governance, such as political polarization, populism, and the role of money in politics.

2. Understanding Authoritarian Systems:

This section delves into the characteristics and mechanisms of authoritarian political systems. We explore the consolidation of power in authoritarian regimes, including the concentration of authority in a single leader or ruling party. We discuss the limitations on civil liberties, the suppression of dissent, and the control of media and information in authoritarian systems. We also analyze the role of propaganda and ideology in maintaining authoritarian rule. Additionally, we examine different types of authoritarianism, such as military juntas, single-party states, and personalistic autocracies.

3. Power Distribution and Accountability:

This section focuses on the contrasting approaches to power distribution and accountability in democratic and authoritarian systems. We explore the separation of powers, checks and balances, and the role of independent institutions in democratic governance. We discuss the mechanisms of accountability, including free and fair elections, judicial oversight, and mechanisms of transparency and anti-corruption. In contrast, we analyze the concentration of power, lack of checks and balances, and the absence of effective accountability mechanisms in authoritarian systems.

4. Protection of Human Rights:

This section examines the implications of democratic and authoritarian systems on human rights. We explore how democratic systems, through their emphasis on individual freedoms, provide a conducive environment for the protection of human rights. We discuss the importance of constitutional safeguards, an independent judiciary, and civil society in upholding human rights in democratic societies. In contrast, we analyze the challenges and violations of human rights in authoritarian systems, such as restrictions on freedom of speech, assembly, and association.

5. Political Stability and Legitimacy:

This section investigates the relationship between political stability and legitimacy in democratic and authoritarian systems. We discuss how democratic systems, through peaceful transitions of power and institutional mechanisms, contribute to political stability. We examine the role of elections, political parties, and public participation in maintaining stability in democracies. In contrast, we analyze the potential vulnerabilities and sources of instability in authoritarian systems, such as succession crises, popular uprisings, and the erosion of public trust.

6. Socioeconomic Development and Governance:

This section explores the implications of democratic and authoritarian systems on socioeconomic development and governance. We examine how democratic systems, through mechanisms of accountability and participation, can contribute to inclusive development, economic growth, and social welfare. We discuss the importance of good governance, transparency, and anti-corruption measures in democratic societies. In contrast, we analyze the challenges and risks of corruption, cronyism, and inequality in authoritarian systems, which can hinder development and lead to societal unrest.

Conclusion:

In the conclusion, we summarize the comparative analysis of democratic and authoritarian systems. We highlight the strengths and weaknesses of each system, their implications for governance, human rights, political stability, and socioeconomic development. By understanding the contrasting features of democratic and authoritarian systems, we gain a deeper appreciation of the challenges and opportunities in designing and implementing effective political systems that meet the aspirations of diverse societies.

Hybrid Regimes: Challenges and Characteristics

In this chapter, we examine hybrid regimes, a unique category of political systems that exhibit elements of both democratic and authoritarian governance. These regimes present a complex and challenging landscape, blurring the lines between democratic institutions and authoritarian practices. Through an analysis of their characteristics, challenges, and dynamics, we aim to understand the implications of hybrid regimes for governance, political stability, and the protection of human rights.

1. Defining Hybrid Regimes:

This section provides a comprehensive definition and understanding of hybrid regimes. We explore the concept of hybridity, highlighting the coexistence of democratic and authoritarian features within these systems. We discuss the challenges associated with categorizing and classifying hybrid regimes, as they often defy traditional labels. Additionally, we provide examples of countries that fall within the hybrid regime spectrum and examine their unique characteristics.

2. Characteristics of Hybrid Regimes:

This section delves into the key characteristics that define hybrid regimes. We explore the manipulation of democratic institutions and processes, including elections, political parties, and media, by those in power. We discuss the presence of limited political competition, restrictions on civil liberties, and the suppression of dissent as common features of hybrid regimes. We also analyze the centralization of power and the erosion of checks and balances within these systems.

3. Political Legitimacy and Hybrid Regimes:

This section explores the challenges of political legitimacy faced by hybrid regimes. We discuss how these regimes often rely on a combination of coercive tactics, manipulation of democratic processes, and control over media to maintain their legitimacy. We examine the strategies employed by hybrid regimes to project an image of popular support while suppressing opposition and dissent. Additionally, we analyze the impact of limited political competition on the legitimacy of hybrid regimes.

4. Implications for Governance and Political Stability:

This section investigates the implications of hybrid regimes for governance and political stability. We examine the challenges faced by hybrid regimes in effectively addressing societal demands, balancing competing interests, and implementing coherent policies. We discuss how the coexistence of democratic and authoritarian elements can lead to policy inconsistency, lack of accountability, and corruption. We also analyze the potential sources of instability within hybrid regimes, including power struggles, social unrest, and challenges to the ruling elite.

5. Human Rights and Hybrid Regimes:

This section examines the implications of hybrid regimes for the protection of human rights. We discuss how these regimes often restrict civil liberties, curtail freedom of speech and assembly, and limit the activities of civil society organizations. We analyze the challenges faced by human rights defenders and the suppression of dissent within hybrid regimes. Additionally, we explore the impact of hybrid regimes on the rule of law, judicial independence, and access to justice.

6. International Engagement and Hybrid Regimes:

This section explores the role of the international community in engaging with hybrid regimes. We discuss the tensions and dilemmas faced by external actors, including states, international organizations, and civil society, when dealing with these regimes. We examine different approaches, such as conditionality, engagement, and sanctions, employed by the international community to influence the behavior of hybrid regimes. We also analyze the challenges of promoting democratic values and human rights while maintaining stability and security in regions with hybrid regimes.

Conclusion:

In the conclusion, we summarize the characteristics and challenges of hybrid regimes. We emphasize the complexity and fluidity of these systems, highlighting the need for nuanced approaches to understand and address the governance issues they present. By examining the hybrid regime phenomenon, we gain insights into the dynamics of political power, the erosion of democratic institutions, and the challenges faced by societies seeking to uphold democratic values in challenging political environments.

In this chapter, we delve into the complex and multifaceted processes of political transitions and democratization. We explore the dynamics, challenges, and outcomes of transitions from authoritarian rule to democratic governance. Through an analysis of historical and contemporary case studies, we aim to understand the factors that contribute to successful democratization and the obstacles that impede progress.

1. Understanding Political Transitions:

This section provides a comprehensive overview of political transitions, examining the reasons why countries undergo transitions from authoritarian rule to democratic governance. We discuss the catalysts for change, including internal and external pressures, societal demands, and shifting power dynamics. Additionally, we analyze the various pathways to political transition, ranging from peaceful negotiations and reforms to revolutionary movements and external interventions.

2. The Role of Leadership:

This section explores the pivotal role of leadership in political transitions and democratization processes. We examine the qualities and strategies of transformative leaders who champion democratic values and institutions.

We analyze the importance of inclusive leadership, coalition-building, and consensus-building in navigating complex political transitions. Additionally, we discuss the challenges faced by leaders in balancing the demands for change with the need for stability and social cohesion.

3. Institutional Reforms:

This section delves into the critical role of institutional reforms in the democratization process. We explore the restructuring of political institutions, including electoral systems, judicial systems, and public administration, to ensure transparency, accountability, and the rule of law. We discuss the challenges of building strong and independent institutions that can withstand political pressures and safeguard democratic values. Additionally, we examine the role of civil society organizations in advocating for institutional reforms and holding governments accountable.

4. Managing Political Violence and Conflict:

This section addresses the challenges of managing political violence and conflict during political transitions. We examine the causes and consequences of violence in transition periods and discuss strategies for reconciliation and peacebuilding. We explore the role of truth and reconciliation commissions, transitional justice mechanisms, and disarmament programs in fostering stability and healing wounds. Additionally, we analyze the challenges of managing competing interests, addressing historical grievances, and preventing the reemergence of violence.

5. Building a Democratic Political Culture:

This section explores the importance of cultivating a democratic political culture during political transitions. We discuss the values, norms, and attitudes that underpin democratic governance, including respect for human rights, pluralism, and participation. We analyze the challenges of instilling democratic values in societies with deep-rooted authoritarian legacies and discuss the role of education, media, and civic engagement in promoting democratic principles. Additionally, we examine the influence of socioeconomic factors, such as inequality and poverty, on the development of a democratic political culture.

6. External Influences on Democratization:

This section examines the role of external actors and influences in the democratization process. We analyze the impact of international organizations, regional bodies, and powerful states in supporting or undermining democratization efforts. We discuss the tensions between the promotion of democratic values and the pursuit of geopolitical interests. Additionally, we explore the challenges of external interventions and the importance of locally driven and context-specific approaches to democratization.

Conclusion:

In the conclusion, we highlight the complexities and challenges of political transitions and democratization processes. We emphasize the need for comprehensive approaches that address political, social, economic, and cultural dimensions of democratization. By understanding the factors that contribute to successful transitions and the obstacles that hinder progress, we can inform and guide future efforts to promote democratic governance worldwide.

Recap of Key Concepts and Insights

In this concluding section, we provide a comprehensive recap of the key concepts, insights, and lessons learned throughout our exploration of global politics, diverse systems, and ideologies. We reflect on the main ideas discussed in each chapter and highlight their significance in understanding the complexities of the global political landscape. By summarizing the key concepts and insights, we aim to reinforce the understanding gained from this exploration and emphasize their relevance in navigating the challenges and prospects of global politics.

1. Understanding Global Politics:

In this subtopic, we revisit the importance of understanding global politics in today's interconnected world. We emphasize the interplay between domestic and international factors, the influence of power dynamics, and the role of ideologies and institutions in shaping global politics. We highlight the significance of informed engagement and the need for a nuanced understanding of diverse political systems and ideologies.

2. Major Political Systems and Ideologies:

In this subtopic, we summarize the main political systems and ideologies discussed throughout the book. We highlight the characteristics, strengths, and weaknesses of democratic governance, authoritarian regimes, and communism. We explore the impact of globalization on political systems and the rise of nationalism and populism. We emphasize the importance of studying and analyzing various ideological perspectives to gain a holistic understanding of global politics.

3. Democratization and Authoritarianism:

In this subtopic, we reflect on the challenges and opportunities associated with democratization processes and the consolidation of power in authoritarian regimes. We highlight the significance of leadership, institutional reforms, and political transitions in fostering democratic governance. We examine the implications for human rights, civil liberties, and political stability in different political systems.

4. Impact of Globalization and International Organizations:

In this subtopic, we discuss the impact of globalization on world politics and the role and significance of international organizations. We explore the challenges and opportunities arising from the interconnectedness of economies, cultures, and societies. We reflect on the tensions between sovereignty and global governance and the need for effective cooperation in addressing global challenges such as climate change, terrorism, and economic inequality.

5. Nationalism, Populism, and Democracy:

In this subtopic, we summarize the rise of nationalist and populist movements and their causes and consequences. We examine the relationship between populism and democracy, highlighting the tensions and potential threats they pose to democratic governance. We discuss the implications for international relations, including the impact on diplomacy, global cooperation, and the balance between national interests and international commitments.

6. Political Ideologies and Movements:

In this subtopic, we recap the origins, principles, and variations of key political ideologies such as liberalism, conservatism, socialism, and other influential perspectives. We explore their impact on governance, social policies, and economic systems. We reflect on the importance of ideological diversity, political discourse, and ideological evolution in shaping the political landscape.

7. Political Systems in Practice:

In this subtopic, we revisit the case studies of political systems worldwide and the comparative analysis of democratic and authoritarian systems. We highlight the characteristics and challenges of hybrid regimes and the complexities of political transitions. We emphasize the importance of context, historical legacies, and societal dynamics in understanding political systems in practice.

Conclusion:

In conclusion, we bring together the key concepts and insights gleaned from our exploration of global politics, diverse systems, and ideologies. We emphasize the importance of understanding the strengths and weaknesses of different political systems, the challenges of democratization, and the impact of globalization. We highlight the role of leadership, institutions, and political culture in shaping governance and the significance of engaging with ideological perspectives. We underscore the need for informed and active engagement in global politics, and the call to address the challenges and prospects for a more inclusive, equitable, and sustainable global order. By integrating these key concepts and insights, we hope to foster a deeper understanding and inspire further exploration of the complex dynamics of global politics.

Challenges and Prospects for Global Politics

In this concluding section, we examine the challenges and prospects that lie ahead in the realm of global politics. Building upon the knowledge and insights gained from our exploration of diverse political systems, ideologies, and actors on the global stage, we delve into the complex issues and potential pathways that shape the future of global governance. By critically analyzing the challenges and envisioning the prospects, we aim to provide a comprehensive understanding of the opportunities and obstacles in the evolving landscape of global politics.

1. Power Shifts and Geopolitical Dynamics:

In this subtopic, we discuss the shifting balance of power and geopolitical dynamics that influence global politics. We examine the rise of emerging powers, changing alliances, and the potential implications for global stability. We explore the challenges posed by power competition, regional conflicts, and the need for effective diplomacy to address complex global issues.

2. Global Governance and Multilateralism:

In this subtopic, we reflect on the role and effectiveness of global governance structures and the significance of multilateralism. We analyze the challenges faced by international organizations in fostering cooperation and addressing global problems such as climate change, economic inequality, and cybersecurity. We explore the potential for reforming existing institutions and the emergence of new mechanisms to tackle pressing global challenges.

3. Technological Advancements and Security:

In this subtopic, we delve into the impact of technological advancements on global politics and the associated security challenges. We examine the role of digitalization, artificial intelligence, and cyber warfare in shaping the international landscape. We address the need for robust cybersecurity measures, ethical frameworks, and global cooperation to mitigate the risks and ensure the responsible use of technology.

4. Inequality and Social Justice:

In this subtopic, we discuss the persistent challenge of inequality and its ramifications for global politics. We analyze the consequences of economic disparities, social exclusion, and unequal distribution of resources. We explore the potential for inclusive economic growth, social welfare policies, and sustainable development initiatives to address these inequalities and foster social justice on a global scale.

5. Environmental Sustainability and Climate Change:

In this subtopic, we reflect on the pressing issue of climate change and its profound implications for global politics. We analyze the challenges of mitigating greenhouse gas emissions, adapting to environmental changes, and promoting sustainable development. We explore the potential for international cooperation, environmental diplomacy, and the role of non-state actors in combating climate change.

6. Rising Nationalism and Populism:

In this subtopic, we address the challenges posed by the rise of nationalism and populism in various parts of the world. We analyze the impact on democratic institutions, human rights, and international relations. We explore strategies for addressing the underlying causes of these movements, fostering dialogue, and promoting inclusive governance models.

7. Digital Divide and Access to Information:

In this subtopic, we examine the digital divide and its implications for global politics. We discuss the challenges of unequal access to information and the potential consequences for democratic participation, human rights, and social cohesion. We explore initiatives aimed at bridging the digital divide, promoting digital literacy, and ensuring equitable access to technology and information resources.

Conclusion:

In conclusion, we have identified and analyzed the significant challenges and prospects that define the landscape of global politics. From power shifts and geopolitical dynamics to environmental sustainability and rising nationalism, these challenges require thoughtful and strategic responses. However, amidst these challenges, there are also prospects for positive change, including the potential for multilateral cooperation, technological advancements, and inclusive governance models. By acknowledging and addressing these challenges while embracing the opportunities, we can navigate the complexities of global politics and work towards a more peaceful, just, and sustainable world. It is through informed engagement, collective action, and a commitment to shared values that we can shape the future of global politics for the better.

Call to Action: Importance of Informed Engagement

In this concluding section, we emphasize the crucial role of informed engagement in shaping the future of global politics. Drawing upon the knowledge and insights gained from our exploration of diverse political systems, ideologies, and actors on the global stage, we highlight the significance of active participation, critical thinking, and informed decision-making by individuals, communities, and societies. By recognizing the power of informed engagement, we can collectively address the challenges, seize the opportunities, and contribute to positive change in the global political landscape.

1. The Power of Informed Engagement:

In this subtopic, we delve into the transformative potential of informed engagement. We discuss how access to accurate information, diverse perspectives, and robust dialogue empowers individuals to make informed choices and actively participate in democratic processes. We explore the importance of media literacy, critical thinking skills, and fact-checking in navigating the complex information landscape and countering misinformation.

2. Strengthening Democratic Institutions:

In this subtopic, we examine the critical role of democratic institutions in fostering informed engagement.

We discuss the need for transparent, accountable, and inclusive governance structures that uphold democratic values, protect civil liberties, and promote citizen participation. We explore the importance of electoral reforms, institutional checks and balances, and grassroots movements in strengthening democratic processes.

3. Promoting Global Citizenship:

In this subtopic, we emphasize the importance of fostering a sense of global citizenship and interconnectedness. We discuss the need for individuals to engage beyond national boundaries, understand diverse cultures and perspectives, and actively contribute to global problem-solving. We explore the potential of educational initiatives, cultural exchange programs, and digital platforms in promoting global awareness and collaboration.

4. Advocacy and Activism:

In this subtopic, we highlight the power of advocacy and activism in driving positive change. We discuss the role of grassroots movements, civil society organizations, and social media in mobilizing public opinion, influencing policy agendas, and holding governments accountable. We explore effective strategies for peaceful protests, lobbying, and engaging with decision-makers to advocate for social justice, human rights, and environmental sustainability.

5. Addressing Inequality and Marginalization:

In this subtopic, we address the urgent need to address inequality and marginalization through informed engagement. We discuss the importance of understanding the root causes of social, economic, and political disparities and advocating for inclusive policies and programs. We explore the potential of community-based initiatives, social entrepreneurship, and inclusive leadership in promoting equality and empowering marginalized groups.

6. Nurturing Intercultural Dialogue and Diplomacy:

In this subtopic, we emphasize the significance of intercultural dialogue and diplomacy in fostering peaceful coexistence and resolving conflicts. We discuss the importance of listening to diverse perspectives, promoting mutual understanding, and finding common ground in addressing global challenges. We explore the role of diplomacy, track-two diplomacy, and cultural diplomacy in bridging differences and promoting cooperation.

7. Harnessing Technology for Positive Change:

In this subtopic, we explore the transformative potential of technology in facilitating informed engagement. We discuss the role of social media, online platforms, and digital tools in amplifying voices, mobilizing communities, and fostering global connections. We address the importance of responsible digital citizenship, online activism, and ethical use of technology in shaping the future of global politics.

Conclusion:

In conclusion, we emphasize the significance of informed engagement as a catalyst for positive change in the global political landscape. By actively participating in democratic processes, advocating for social justice, promoting global citizenship, and harnessing the power of technology, individuals and communities can shape a more equitable, inclusive, and sustainable world. It is through our collective efforts, informed by knowledge, empathy, and a commitment to shared values, that we can overcome the challenges and seize the opportunities presented by global politics. Let us be proactive, engaged global citizens, working together to build a better future for all.

THE END

To help you better understand the language and concepts related to aging and older adults, below you will find a list of key terms and their definitions.

key terms

1. Global Politics: The study of political systems, ideologies, and actors on the global stage and their interactions with one another.

2. Political Systems: The structures, processes, and institutions through which political power is organized, exercised, and distributed within a society or among nations.

3. Ideologies: Sets of beliefs, values, and ideas that shape political and social thought, guiding individuals and groups in their understanding of the world and their vision for society.

4. Actors: Individuals, groups, organizations, and states that play a role in shaping and influencing global politics, including governments, international organizations, non-governmental organizations (NGOs), and multinational corporations.

5. Democratic Governance: A system of government in which power is vested in the people, who exercise it directly or through elected representatives. It is characterized by

principles such as political participation, rule of law, transparency, and respect for human rights.

6. Authoritarian Regimes: Political systems in which power is concentrated in the hands of a single leader or a small group, often characterized by limited political freedoms, suppression of dissent, and a lack of checks and balances.

7. Communism: A political ideology and socioeconomic system characterized by the common ownership of the means of production and the absence of social classes, aiming for a classless society where resources are distributed based on need.

8. Globalization: The process of increasing interconnectedness and interdependence among countries through the exchange of goods, services, information, and ideas, leading to the emergence of a globalized world.

9. International Organizations: Institutions created by states to facilitate cooperation and address global challenges, such as the United Nations, World Trade Organization, and International Monetary Fund.

10. Nationalism: A political ideology that emphasizes the interests and identity of a particular nation, often advocating for self-determination, sovereignty, and the protection of national interests.

11. Populism: A political approach that seeks to appeal to the interests and sentiments of ordinary people, often by presenting themselves as representing the "true" voice of the people against established elites.

12. Liberalism: A political ideology that emphasizes individual freedoms, equal rights, representative democracy, and the protection of civil liberties.

13. Conservatism: A political ideology that emphasizes the preservation of traditional values, social order, and limited government intervention.

14. Socialism: A political ideology advocating for collective ownership and control of resources, as well as the pursuit of social and economic equality.

15. Hybrid Regimes: Political systems that combine elements of both democracy and authoritarianism, often characterized by flawed elections, restricted civil liberties, and a lack of institutional accountability.

Supporting Materials

Introduction

No specific references required for the introduction.

Chapter 1: Democratic Governance

Dahl, R. A. (2000). On democracy. Yale University Press.

Chapter 2: Authoritarian Regimes

Levitsky, S., & Way, L. A. (2010). Competitive authoritarianism: Hybrid regimes after the Cold War. Cambridge University Press.

Chapter 3: The Evolution of Communism

Marx, K., & Engels, F. (1848). The communist manifesto. Penguin Classics.

Suny, R. G. (1993). The Soviet experiment: Russia, the USSR, and the successor states. Oxford University Press.

Chapter 4: Globalization and International Organizations

Held, D., McGrew, A., Goldblatt, D., & Perraton, J. (1999). Global transformations: Politics, economics and culture. Polity Press.

Chapter 5: Nationalism and Populism

Judis, J. B. (2016). The populist explosion: How the great recession transformed American and European politics. Columbia Global Reports.

Chapter 6: Political Ideologies and Movements

Heywood, A. (2017). Political ideologies: An introduction. Palgrave Macmillan.

Chapter 7: Political Systems in Practice

Diamond, L., & Morlino, L. (Eds.). (2005). Assessing the quality of democracy. JHU Press.

Conclusion

No specific references required for the conclusion.

www.ingramcontent.com/pod-product-compliance
Lightning Source LLC
LaVergne TN
LVHW020334200726
843507LV00012B/2355